MONEY SAVING
MEALS & ROUND 2
RECIPES

Sandra Lee

MONEY SAVING
MEALS & ROUND 2
RECIPES

This book belongs to:

_____

SL BOOKS
sandralee.com

HYPERION
NEW YORK

LIBRARY OF CONGRESS CATALOGING-IN-PUBLICATION DATA

Lee, Sandra.

    Money saving meals and round 2 recipes / Sandra Lee.

       p. cm.

    ISBN 978-1-4013-1081-3 (pbk.)

1. Quick and easy cooking. 2. Cooking—United States. 3. Cookbooks. I. Title.

    TX833.5.L3965 2011

    641.5'52—dc23   2011022419

Hyperion books are available for special promotions and premiums. For details contact the HarperCollins Special Markets Department in the New York office at 212-207-7528, fax 212-207-7222, or email spsales@harpercollins.com.

Photographs by BEN FINK
Food styling by JAMIE KIMM
Prop styling by DANI FISHER

FIRST EDITION

10 9 8 7 6 5 4 3 2 1

THIS LABEL APPLIES TO TEXT STOCK

We try to produce the most beautiful books possible, and we are also extremely concerned about the impact of our manufacturing process on the forests of the world and the environment as a whole. Accordingly, we've made sure that all of the paper we use has been certified as coming from forests that are managed, to ensure the protection of the people and wildlife dependent upon them.

To all the families struggling to make ends meet while striving to put healthful delicious meals on the table

Contents

A LETTER FROM SANDRA — viii

1. A HEARTY HELPING — 2

2. THE GREAT FOOD GATHERING — 12

3. BRILLIANT BASEMENT BARGAINS — 24

4. BIG EASY DINNER — 34

5. CHEAPER BY THE DOZEN — 44

6. THE FAMILY KITCHEN — 52

7. FIESTA CUISINE CLASSICS — 66

8. FARM STAND FRESH — 76

9. FEEDING A CROWD — 88

10. GERMAN FAMILY-FEST — 100

11. GRILLING ON A STICK — 110

12. AFFORDABLE EASY ENTERTAINING — 122

13. BRUNCH FOR A BUNCH   134

14. A BOUNTIFUL HARVEST   148

15. THE HOLIDAY HELPER   164

16. LESS IS MORE   178

17. MORE THAN MEAT AND POTATOES   188

18. PERFECT PASTA PLATES   198

19. FROM THE MEDITERRANEAN   210

20. MINUTE MEAL MAGIC   220

21. GOING GLOBAL WITH THAI   230

22. COMFORTING SOUL FOOD   240

23. THRIFTY TEX MEX   250

24. FLASH IN THE PAN   262

25. SMART, SIMPLE SERVING   274

INDEX   284

A Letter from Sandra

Money Saving Meals & Round 2 Recipes hosts an abundance of magical meals made in minutes. The recipes you'll find here are great for your pocketbook, your daily schedule, your to-do list, and your family's healthful nourishment.

There are very few occasions where you can make something fast and also save money. My goal with the *Money Saving Meals* Food Network show and this book is to give you both—fabulous, fast, budget-conscious food for everyday cooking, and healthy meals that take minutes to make and that you'll be proud to feed your family.

When I created *Money Saving Meals,* my goal was to save you 25% on every grocery store bill. However, with the investment of a great deal of research, shopping know-how, and pantry-perfect products (which allow multipurpose uses), I will save you 35% to 50%, on average.

Money Saving Meals has launched with a bang. What does that say? We all want to save money without sacrificing quality, quantity, or style—and that is exactly what this cookbook delivers.

Here is the short list to saving big dollars:

1. **Check Sales**: The first of the month, name-brand products go on sale, and at the end of the month, private-label products go on sale.
2. **Club Stores**: Sam's Club, Costco, and BJ's have membership fees that cost around $50 annually, but you should save that on your very first purchase. Club stores make their money on their membership fees, not product margins.
3. **Couponing**: See Sunday Supplements for the best coupon clippings, and use them when the store sales go up—you'll double your savings.

You never have to pay a fortune to feed your family first class if you have the know-how and knowledge. Cheers to a happy, healthy home,

MONEY SAVING
MEALS & ROUND 2
RECIPES

1. A HEARTY HELPING

- **Meal total: $26.37/$6.59 per person**
  Slow Cooker Short Ribs, Mushroom
  Walnut Tarts, and Ginger Spice Cake
  with Ginger Glaze

1. Slow Cooker Short Ribs

Total cost: 18.37/$4.59 per person

Save 76% by chopping your own carrots and onions instead of buying them pre-chopped

Using spicy brown mustard instead of Dijon will save you 53%

2. Mushroom Walnut Tarts

Total cost: $4.06/$1.02 per person

Frozen Vegetable Individual Tarts cost 22% more than Sandra's

Beef broth costs the same as vegetable broth and adds more flavor

3. Ginger Spice Cake with Ginger Glaze

Total cost: $3.94/$0.49 per person

Buy your applesauce in a jar and save 33% over individual cups

4. R2R: Beef and Mushroom Soup

$0.00 in extra ingredients

Veal bone in shanks = $8.99/lb
Bone in Short Ribs = $4.49/serving
Savings = $4.50 or 50%

TART SHELLS
Puff Pastry Individual Shells = $0.77/serving
Pie Crust Mix = $0.06/serving
Savings = $0.17 or 92%

GINGER SPICE CAKE
Bakery Ginger Spice Cake = $9.99
SL Homemade Ginger Cake = $3.94
Savings = $6.05 or 61%

BAKING MIX
Store-bought Baking Mix = $0.30/cup
Sandra's Baking Mix = $0.15/cup
Savings = $0.15 or 50%

BEEF AND MUSHROOM SOUP
Store-bought Can of Beef and Vegetable Soup = $1.75/serving
SL Homemade Beef and Mushroom Soup = $0.00
Savings = $1.75 or 100%

SLOW COOKER SHORT RIBS

1	tbsp. canola oil	$0.03
3	pounds bone-in beef chuck short ribs	$13.47
2	medium onions, peeled and quartered	$0.56
2	medium carrots, cut into large chunks	$0.32
2	medium parsnips, cut into large chunks	$1.00
2	medium turnips, peeled and cut into large chunks	$1.00
4	sprigs fresh rosemary	$0.04
4	sprigs fresh thyme	$0.04
4	sprigs fresh parsley, stems and leaves separated	$0.02
1	tbsp. Worcestershire sauce	$0.02
1	tbsp. spicy brown mustard	$0.04
1	(12-ounce) dark stout beer, such as Guinness	$1.83
	Kosher salt	$0.00
	Black pepper	$0.00

In a large skillet over medium-high heat, add the oil. Season the short ribs with salt and pepper. When the oil is hot, brown the short ribs, in batches, until they are browned on all sides, about 3–4 minutes per side.

While the short ribs are browning, place a layer of onion and carrot pieces into the bottom of a slow cooker and season them with salt and pepper. Place the browned meat on top. Add the remaining onions and carrots along with the parsnips and turnips. Tie together the rosemary and thyme with the parsley stems and add them to the pot along with the Worcestershire and mustard. Pour over the stout and add enough water to almost cover the contents. Cover and cook on low for 6–8 hours, or until the meat is very tender.

To serve, carefully remove the meat and vegetables from the slow cooker. Strain the juices. (Skim off the fat and reserve 1 cup of the juices and one short rib for Round 2 Recipe: Beef and Mushroom Soup.) Serve the ribs with the juice and garnish with chopped parsley leaves.

SERVES: 4
COOK TIME: 8 hours
$18.37/$4.59 per person

Please see Round 2 Recipe on page 10

MUSHROOM WALNUT TARTS

½	package piecrust mix	$0.45
1	tbsp. canola oil	$0.03
1	medium diced onion	$0.28
2	tsp. minced garlic	$0.02
1	(8-ounce) package sliced mushrooms	$1.99
2	tsp. fresh chopped thyme	$0.02
¼	cup chopped walnuts	$0.43
¼	cup bread crumbs	$0.05
1	(14-ounce) can beef broth	$0.79
	Kosher salt, to taste	$0.00
	Black pepper, to taste	$0.00

Preheat oven to 375°F.

Prepare piecrust mix according to package instructions. Divide between 10 cups of a muffin tin, pressing in bottom and up sides in an even layer. Refrigerate while preparing the filling.

Heat canola oil in a large skillet over medium-high heat. Add onion, garlic, sliced mushrooms, thyme. Season with salt and pepper to taste. Sauté until mushrooms are golden. Set aside 10 mushroom slices to top tarts. (Set aside ⅓ cup mushrooms and onions for Round 2 Recipe: Beef and Mushroom Soup.)

Add remaining sautéed mushrooms and onions with walnuts into bowl of food processor fitted with a blade attachment. Pulse to coarsely chop. Add bread crumbs and ¼ cup beef broth. (Reserve remaining beef broth for Round 2 Recipe: Beef and Mushroom Soup.)

Spoon mushroom and walnut mixture into piecrust-lined muffin tins. Top each with a sliced mushroom. Bake in oven for 20–25 minutes, or until crust is golden. Remove from oven and cool in pan before carefully removing tarts.

SERVES: 4
MAKES: 10 tarts
COOK TIME: 25 minutes
$4.06/$1.02 per person

Please see Round 2 Recipe on page 10

GINGER SPICE CAKE WITH GINGER GLAZE

3	tbsp. grated ginger (from about 3″ piece of ginger)	$0.36
2	cups all-purpose flour	$0.28
1	tsp. baking powder	$0.02
½	tsp. baking soda	$0.01
1	tbsp. pumpkin pie spice	$0.90
1	cup packed brown sugar	$0.35
1	cup applesauce	$0.56
½	cup canola oil	$0.24
1	egg	$0.11
1	tsp. vanilla extract	$0.44
1	cup powdered sugar	$0.24
¼	cup chopped walnuts	$0.43

Preheat oven to 350°F. Spray an 8-inch cake pan with nonstick cooking spray.

Place grated ginger in two layers of cheesecloth, or two layers of paper towel. Squeeze to extract juice from zest and set aside for glaze.

In a large bowl whisk together the baking mix with pumpkin pie spice and juiced grated ginger.

In a separate bowl whisk together the brown sugar, applesauce, canola oil, egg, and vanilla until well combined. Stir together the wet ingredients into the dry ingredients until thoroughly incorporated. Scrape batter into prepared cake pan leveling top with a spatula. Bake for 40–45 minutes or until toothpick inserted in center comes out mostly clean with a few crumbs clinging to it. Remove from oven, when cool enough to handle invert cake onto a wire cooling rack.

For glaze, stir together the powdered sugar with ginger juice and just enough water to form a pourable but very thick consistency. When cake is completely cool, while still on wire rack, make a thin horizontal cut through top to partially level the cake. Flip cake over so bottom side is up. Pour glaze onto center, use an off-set spatula to help the glaze run down the sides. Sprinkle the edges with chopped walnuts to garnish.

SERVES: 8
COOK TIME: 35 minutes
$3.94/$0.49 per person

BEEF AND MUSHROOM SOUP

Leftover drippings from Slow Cooker Short Ribs	$0.00
⅓ cup leftover mushroom and onions from Mushroom Walnut Tarts	$0.00
1½ cups leftover beef broth from Mushroom Walnut Tarts	$0.00
Leftover rib from Slow Cooker Short Ribs, meat removed and coarsely chopped	$0.00

In a medium pot over medium heat add drippings from short ribs. Add leftover mushroom and onions. Bring to a simmer. Stir in beef broth and two cups water. Bring to a simmer, then stir in leftover meat.

SERVES: 2

COOK TIME: 10 minutes

$0.00 in extra ingredients

Please see Main Recipes on pages 4 and 6

2. THE GREAT FOOD GATHERING

- Every once in a while you want to treat your family to a special meal, but not if it is going to cost you a fortune.
- **Meal total: $23.34/$5.84 per person**
  Ginger and Brown Sugar Glazed Ham,
  Carrot and Parsnip Au Gratin, Pineapple
  Pudding Cakes, and Pineapple Paradise

1. Ginger and Brown Sugar Glazed Ham
Total cost: $14.50/$3.63 per person

Using brown sugar saves 89% a cup instead of honey

MSM TIP:
Spiral Glazed Ham = $3.29/lb
Whole Smoked Ham = $1.89/lb
Savings = $1.40 or 43%

2. Carrot and Parsnip Au Gratin
Total cost: $5.82/$1.46 per person

Using Sandra's homemade béchamel sauce will save you 30% instead of store-bought cream sauce

Save 46% when you buy your carrots in a 5-pound bag instead of a 1-pound bag

MSM TIP 2:
Store-bought Glaze = $4.79
SL Glaze = $1.27
Savings = $3.52 or 73%

3. Pineapple Pudding Cakes
Total cost: $1.60/$0.40 per person

Canned pineapple chunks cost 75% less than fresh pineapple chunks at the market

MSM TIP:
Heavy Cream = $2.24
Sandra's Béchamel = $0.52
Savings = $1.72 or 77%

4. Pineapple Paradise
Total cost: $1.42/$0.36 per serving

5. R2R: Ham Skillet Casserole
$0.75 in extra ingredients

GINGER AND BROWN SUGAR GLAZED HAM

1	7-pound smoked fresh ham	$13.23
½	cup packed light brown sugar	$0.18
½	cup apple jelly	$0.69
1	tbsp. finely grated fresh ginger	$0.12
2	tsp. minced garlic	$0.03
¼	cup spicy brown mustard	$0.16
3	tbsp. apple cider vinegar	$0.09

Preheat oven to 350°F. Place ham in a roasting pan fat-side up. Score fat with a crisscross pattern and cover with foil. Cook ham for about 1½ hours or until a meat thermometer inserted in the center reads 145°F.

In the meantime, in a small saucepan over medium heat stir together remaining ingredients for glaze along with 2 tablespoons water. Bring to a simmer and cook for about 2 minutes until it has a smooth syrupy consistency.

Remove ham from oven. Pour off liquid in pan, generously coat ham with half of the glaze. Place in oven and bake an additional 20–30 minutes, halfway through basting with remaining glaze. Remove from oven and allow ham to rest for 30 minutes before slicing and serving. (Reserve 1 cup ham for Round 2 Recipe: Ham Skillet Casserole.)

SERVES: 4
COOK TIME: 2 hours
$14.50/$3.63 per person

Please see Round 2 Recipe on page 22

CARROT AND PARSNIP AU GRATIN

5	large carrots, sliced on the bias ¼" thick	$0.80
5	large parsnips, sliced on the bias ¼" thick	$2.50
2	tbsp. butter	$0.12
1	tbsp. canola oil	$0.03
1	tbsp. minced garlic	$0.05
¼	cup flour	$0.04
2½	cups milk	$0.40
3	sprigs fresh thyme	$0.03
¼	tsp. pumpkin pie spice	$0.08
1	cup grated Cheddar cheese	$1.00
1	cup bread crumbs	$0.19
2	tbsp. fresh chopped parsley	$0.04
¼	cup grated Parmesan cheese	$0.54
	Kosher salt, to taste	$0.00
	Black pepper, to taste	$0.00

In a medium saucepan over medium heat melt the butter with canola oil. Add the garlic and cook 1 minute. Add the flour and cook stirring constantly until the flour is lightly golden brown, about 2 minutes. Slowly whisk in the milk and add sprigs of thyme. Bring mixture to a simmer and cook until very thick. Remove thyme stems from pot and stir in the Cheddar cheese, pumpkin pie spice, and salt and pepper to taste.

Coat the bottom of baking dish with a thin layer of the béchamel sauce. Place one layer of carrots slightly overlapping in the bottom of the baking dish. Top with an overlapping layer of the parsnips. Pour ⅓ of the béchamel sauce over top. Repeat with 2 more layers each of the carrots and parsnips, ending with the béchamel sauce.

In a small bowl stir together the bread crumbs with parsley, Parmesan cheese, and salt and pepper to taste.

Bake for 1 hour 30 minutes or until gratin is bubbling and the topping is browned, and when pierced-through vegetables yield easily.

(Reserve 1 cup of Carrot and Parsnip Au Gratin for Round 2 Recipe: Ham Skillet Casserole.)

SERVES: 4
COOK TIME: 1 hour 30 minutes
$5.82/$1.46 per person

Please see Round 2 Recipe on page 22

PINEAPPLE PUDDING CAKES

2	eggs	$0.22
¼	cup sugar	$0.05
1	(8-ounce) can pineapple chunks	$0.99
½	cup skim milk	$0.08
½	tsp. vanilla extract	$0.22
¼	cup all-purpose flour	$0.04
¼	tsp. kosher salt	$0.00

Preheat the oven to 325°F. Place a full tea kettle over medium-low heat. Spray 4 (1-cup) oven-proof ramekins with nonstick cooking spray.

Drain can of pineapple well, reserving ¼ cup of juice for Pineapple Paradise cocktail, page 20. Set aside the pineapple chunks.

Separate the eggs, putting the whites in a slightly larger bowl. Using a hand mixer whip the egg whites until they hold stiff peaks, set aside. To the yolks, add the sugar and beat until the sugar is dissolved and the color has turned a pale yellow. Add the pineapple juice. Sift in the flour and salt and mix well. Mix in milk.

Fold the whites into the yolk mixture. Divide the batter among the ramekins. Place the ramekins into a baking dish and pour in hot water until it reaches halfway up the sides of the ramekins. Bake the pudding cakes for 20–22 minutes until set. Let cool to room temperature before inverting onto plates. To serve, garnish with pineapple chunks. (Reserve 8 pieces pineapple for Pineapple Paradise cocktail, page 20.)

SERVES: 4
COOK TIME: 24 minutes
$1.60/$0.40 per person

PINEAPPLE PARADISE

¼	cup reserved juice from Pineapple Pudding Cakes	$0.00
1	2"-piece of thinly sliced ginger	$0.24
¼	cup sugar	$0.05
2	cups pineapple juice	$0.80
1	liter sparkling water	$0.33
	Reserved pineapple chunks from Pineapple Pudding Cakes for garnish	$0.00
4	ounces spiced rum (optional)	$1.60

In a small saucepan over medium heat, stir together the reserved juice from can of crushed pineapple, with ¼ cup sugar and ginger slices. Bring to a simmer to dissolve sugar, remove from heat and allow to cool to room temperature.

In a large pitcher stir together the pineapple ginger simple syrup with 2 cans of pineapple juice and rum, if using. Pour into ice-filled glasses and top off each with sparkling water. Garnish each with two pineapple chunks on a toothpick.

SERVES: 4
$1.42/$0.36 per person

HAM SKILLET CASSEROLE

1	cup reserved gratin from Carrot and Parsnip Au Gratin	$0.00
1	cup reserved ham from Ginger and Brown Sugar Glazed Ham	$0.00
4	eggs	$0.44
1	cup milk	$0.16
½	cup baking mix	$0.15
	Kosher salt, to taste	$0.00
	Black pepper, to taste	$0.00

Preheat oven to 350°F. Spray a 9-inch ovenproof skillet with nonstick cooking spray.

In a large bowl whisk together the eggs with the milk and baking mix. Stir in the reserved gratin and ham. Heat skillet over medium heat. Pour the mixture into the skillet. Stir gently until it begins to set up. Place in oven and continue to cook until center is firm and top is golden, about 20 minutes.

SERVES: 4
COOK TIME: 25 minutes
$0.75/$0.19 per person

Please see Main Recipes on pages 14 and 16

3. BRILLIANT BASEMENT BARGAINS

- Terrific brunch classics without breaking a sweat or putting a dent in the family budget.
- **Meal total: $15.95/$3.99 per person**
  Eggs Benedict, Ham and Cheese Soufflé, Coffee Cake, and Bloody Mary

1. Eggs Benedict
Total cost: $5.87/$1.47 per person

2. Ham and Cheese Soufflé
Total cost: $3.90/$0.98 per person

Use canola oil here instead of butter, because it saves 50% and you won't be sacrificing any flavor.

3. Coffee Cake
Total cost: $3.37/$0.42 per person

4. Bloody Mary
Total cost: $2.81/$0.70 per person

5. R2R: Savory Bread Pudding with Ham
$1.02 in extra ingredients

6. R2R: Eggs in Purgatory
$2.38 in extra ingredients

EGGS BENEDICT

8	eggs	$0.88
1	tbsp. white vinegar	$0.01
1	tbsp. vegetable oil	$0.03
16	slices bacon	$2.72
8	slices whole wheat bread, toasted	$1.05

HOLLANDAISE SAUCE:

½	cup butter, melted	$0.74
3	eggs, separated	$0.33
1	tsp. fresh lemon juice	$0.06
1	tsp. Worcestershire sauce	$0.02
1	tbsp. chopped fresh parsley	$0.02
	Kosher salt, to taste	$0.00
	Pinch cayenne pepper	$0.01

SERVES: 4
COOK TIME: 18 minutes
$5.87/$1.47 per person

Preheat oven to 400°F. Line a sheet pan with bacon slices and bake for 15 minutes.

Fill a large, deep-sided skillet ¾ of the way up with water. Bring to a light simmer over low heat and add the vinegar.

Use a biscuit cutter to cut 8 slices of toasted bread into rounds. (Reserve the crust for the Round 2 Recipe: Savory Bread Pudding with Ham, page 32.)

Crack the eggs one at a time into a small dish or ramekin and slide each into lightly simmering water. Using a slotted spoon, carefully corral the white of each egg around its yolk. Poach eggs about 2–3 minutes, until the white is set but the yolk is still runny in the middle. Remove eggs onto a paper towel–lined plate.

Separate 3 eggs. (Reserve 3 egg whites for Ham and Cheese Soufflé, page 28.)

In a blender, place egg yolks, lemon juice, and Worcestershire sauce. Pulse until combined, then on medium speed slowly pour in the melted butter through the hole in the blender lid. Season with salt and cayenne pepper.

TO ASSEMBLE:

Place 2 slices of toast on each plate. Break the bacon strips in half and place four halves on each toast round, then a poached egg. Slowly pour the hollandaise sauce over each egg to coat, and sprinkle with chopped parsley.

Please see Round 2 Recipe on page 32

HAM AND CHEESE SOUFFLÉ

3	tbsp. canola oil	$0.09
3	tbsp. flour	$0.01
1½	cups milk, warmed	$0.32
1	tbsp. Dijon mustard	$0.08
3	large eggs, separated, plus 3 reserved egg whites from Eggs Benedict (page 26)	$0.33
6	ounces shredded sharp Cheddar	$1.41
⅓	pound deli ham, diced	$1.66
½	tsp. kosher salt	$0.00

Preheat oven to 375°F. Spray four 7-ounce ramekins with nonstick spray. Heat canola oil over medium-high heat in a medium saucepan. Add flour, whisking constantly, about 3 minutes, avoiding browning. Add warmed milk and whisk until thickened, about 3 more minutes. Remove from heat and slightly cool. Whisk in egg yolks one at a time, then add cheese and ham. (Reserve ⅓ cup of ham for Round 2 Recipe: Savory Bread Pudding with Ham, page 32.)

In another bowl with an electric mixer, beat egg whites until soft peaks form. Add ¼ of the egg whites to the mixture to lighten, then fold in the rest of the whites. Add to soufflé dish, and bake 25–30 minutes until puffed up and browned.

SERVES: 4
COOK TIME: 40 minutes
$3.90/$0.98 per person

Please see Round 2 Recipe on page 32

COFFEE CAKE

2	sticks unsalted butter	$1.00
2¾	cups sugar	$0.48
2	eggs	$0.22
1	cup sour cream	$0.38
1	tsp. vanilla extract	$0.44
2	cups flour	$0.28
1	tbsp. baking powder	$0.04
1	tbsp. cinnamon	$0.48
1	tbsp. brown sugar	$0.02
2	tbsp. confectioners' sugar	$0.03
¼	tsp. kosher salt	$0.00

Preheat oven to 350°F.

Spray a springform cake pan or Bundt pan with nonstick spray.

Using an electric mixer, cream together butter and 2 cups of sugar. Add eggs one at a time, then add sour cream and vanilla extract and mix until blended. In a separate bowl, mix together flour, baking powder, and salt. Mix dry ingredients into wet ingredients until just blended.

In another small bowl, combine remaining ¾ cup sugar, brown sugar, and cinnamon.

Pour half of the batter into the cake pan. Sprinkle with half of the cinnamon sugar mixture. Add remaining batter to pan and top with the rest of the cinnamon sugar. Bake 50–60 minutes, or until a cake tester comes out clean. Let cool slightly and sift confectioners' sugar over the top.

SERVES: 4
COOK TIME: 50 minutes
$3.37/$0.42 per person

BLOODY MARY

4	cups tomato juice	$1.28
	Juice of 1 lemon	$0.50
2	tsp. Worcestershire sauce	$0.04
1	tbsp. hot sauce	$0.06
1	tbsp. Cajun seasoning	$0.33
4	stalks celery, with leaves attached	$0.60
6	ounces vodka	$3.18
	Kosher salt, to taste, plus 1 tbsp. for rimming the glasses	$0.00
	Black pepper, to taste	$0.00

Combine 1 tablespoon of salt and Cajun seasoning on a small plate and mix well. Dip rim of each glass in water, then into the seasoning.

In a pitcher, combine the tomato juice, lemon juice, Worcestershire sauce, and hot sauce. (Reserve 1½ cups of mixture for Round 2 Recipe: Eggs in Purgatory, page 33.) Season with salt and pepper. Fill glasses with ice cubes and add 1½ ounces of vodka to each. Top off with Bloody Mary mix and garnish with celery stalk.

SERVES: 4
$2.81/$0.70 per person

Please see Round 2 Recipe on page 33

SAVORY BREAD PUDDING WITH HAM

1	tbsp. canola oil	$0.03
1	medium yellow onion	$0.28
2	sprigs fresh thyme, leaves only	$0.02
	Leftover bread crusts from Eggs Benedict (page 26) plus 2 slices of toasted whole wheat bread	$0.26
	Leftover diced ham (page 28)	$0.00
4	large eggs	$0.44
2	cups milk	$0.32
	Kosher salt, to taste	$0.00
	Black pepper, to taste	$0.00

Preheat oven to 375°F.

Cut leftover bread crusts and whole wheat toast into cubes. Heat canola oil over medium heat and add onion. Sauté until softened and golden, about 5 minutes. Add thyme leaves, salt and pepper to taste, and set aside. Place all bread in a 9 × 13-inch baking dish. Pour onion mixture over. Add diced ham and toss to combine.

In a separate bowl, whisk together eggs with milk and season with salt and pepper. Pour egg mixture over the bread mixture. Let mixture sit to absorb liquid, about 15 minutes. Bake for 30–35 minutes, until top is golden brown and middle is set.

SERVES: 4
PREP TIME: 10 minutes
COOK TIME: 35 minutes
$1.02 in extra ingredients

Please see Main Recipes on pages 26 and 28

EGGS IN PURGATORY

1	tbsp. canola oil	$0.03
1	medium yellow onion, diced	$0.28
1	tsp. fresh minced garlic	$0.02
1	(14-ounce) can crushed tomatoes	$0.70
1½	cups leftover Bloody Mary mix (page 31)	$0.00
½	tsp. crushed red pepper	$0.04
1	tbsp. chopped fresh basil	$0.02
4	eggs	$0.44
4	slices crusty bread, toasted in oven	$0.85
	Kosher salt, to taste	$0.00

Heat oil in a skillet over medium heat. Add onion and sauté until soft, about 5 minutes. Add garlic and cook 1 more minute. Add crushed tomatoes and Bloody Mary mix, and season with salt and crushed red pepper. Let simmer 5 minutes, then add basil.

Crack the eggs into the tomato sauce and cook until the whites are set and the yolks are still runny. Turn off heat. Toast slices of crusty bread and serve an egg over each slice. Serve with more sauce.

SERVES: 4
COOK TIME: 18 minutes
$2.38 in extra ingredients

Please see Main Recipe on page 31

4. BIG EASY DINNER

- Celebrate the flavors of New Orleans at a price that feels like Mardi Gras.
- New Orleans is one of the most famous American cities for its cuisine; and with a little know-how and some good techniques, I'll show you how to get those flavors into your own kitchen and save yourself a lot of money in the process.
- **Meal #1 total: $15.23/$3.81 per person**
  - Cajun Catfish Cakes with Creamy Remoulade, Gentle Hurricane Cocktail, and Cherries Jubilee Ice Cream Parfait
- **Meal #2 total: $15.13/$3.78 per person**
  - Chicken Jambalaya, Gentle Hurricane Cocktail, and Cherries Jubilee Ice Cream Parfait

---

1. Cajun Catfish Cakes with Creamy Remoulade

Total cost: $9.34/$2.34 per person

2. Chicken Jambalaya

Total cost: $9.24/$2.30 per person

3. Gentle Hurricane Cocktail

Total cost: $1.97/$0.49 per person

4. Cherries Jubilee Ice Cream Parfait

Total cost: $3.92/$0.98 per person

5. R2R: Cajun Quesadilla

$1.78 in extra ingredients

6. R2R: Cajun Red Bean and Rice Soup

$2.74 in extra ingredients

CAJUN CATFISH CAKES WITH CREAMY REMOULADE

4	catfish fillets, about 6 ounces each	$7.49
1	tbsp. plus 1 tsp. Cajun seasoning	$0.44
1	cup canola oil	$0.48
1	cup mayonnaise	$0.47
1	tsp. chopped garlic	$0.02
2	tsp. hot sauce	$0.04
1	tsp. lemon juice	$0.08
1	large beaten egg	$0.11
2	tbsp. spicy brown mustard	$0.08
1	cup cracker crumbs	$0.13
	Kosher salt, to taste	$0.00
	Black pepper, to taste	$0.00

Preheat grill pan over medium-high heat.

Season the catfish on both sides with 1 tablespoon Cajun seasoning and salt and pepper to taste. Brush the grill pan with some of the canola oil, and grill catfish until cooked through, about 4–5 minutes on each side. Remove to a plate and let cool.

While the fish is cooking, make the remoulade: In a bowl, stir together the mayonnaise (set aside 2 table-spoons for the catfish cakes), 1 teaspoon Cajun seasoning, garlic, hot sauce, and lemon juice. (Reserve ½ cup remoulade for Round 2 Recipe: Cajun Quesadilla, page 42.)

Flake the fish into a bowl and add the egg, reserved mayonnaise, mustard, and cracker crumbs. Fold every-thing together. Form into 8 small cakes and set aside.

In a large skillet over medium heat, add the remaining canola oil. When it is hot, add the catfish cakes and cook until browned on each side, about 4–5 minutes. Drain on brown paper. Serve with remoulade.

SERVES: 4
COOK TIME: 15 minutes
$9.34/$2.34 per person

Please see Round 2 Recipe on page 42

CHICKEN JAMBALAYA

2	tbsp. canola oil	$0.06
1½	pounds boneless, skinless chicken thighs, cut into bite-size pieces	$4.49
1	medium yellow chopped onion	$0.28
1	chopped green bell pepper	$0.89
2	chopped stalks celery	$0.30
1	tbsp. chopped garlic	$0.05
1	tbsp. Cajun seasoning	$0.33
¼	tsp. cayenne pepper	$0.03
2	cups long grain rice	$0.60
3	cups chicken broth	$1.20
1	(14-ounce) can diced tomatoes, with juice	$0.99
1	tbsp. chopped fresh parsley	$0.02
	Kosher salt, to taste	$0.00
	Black pepper, to taste	$0.00

In a large heavy-bottomed pot over medium-high heat, add the oil. Season chicken lightly with salt and pepper, and brown on both sides, about 5 minutes per side, working in batches if necessary.

Remove the chicken to a plate. Add the onion, pepper, and celery, and cook until the vegetables are soft and beginning to brown, about 6–8 minutes. Stir in the garlic, Cajun seasoning, cayenne, salt, and pepper.

Return the chicken to the pot. (Remove 1 cup chicken and vegetable mixture for Round 2 Recipe: Cajun Quesadilla, page 42.)

Stir in the rice, add the broth and tomatoes, and season with salt and pepper. Bring to a boil, cover, and reduce heat to simmer. Cook until the liquid is absorbed and the rice is tender, about 30 minutes. (Reserve 2 cups of rice mixture for Round 2 Recipe: Cajun Red Bean and Rice Soup, page 42.) Serve garnished with parsley.

SERVES: 4
COOK TIME: 45 minutes
$9.24/$2.30 per person

Please see Round 2 Recipes on page 42

GENTLE HURRICANE COCKTAIL

2	cups orange juice	$0.64
2	cups pineapple juice	$0.80
4	maraschino cherries, plus ½ cup juice	$0.28
½	orange, cut into 4 slices	$0.25
4	ounces dark rum, optional	$2.28

In a pitcher, stir together the orange juice, pineapple juice, and cherry juice. Fill tall glasses with ice, pour over the juice mixture, and garnish with a cherry and a slice of orange. For the adults, add 1 ounce dark rum to each drink.

SERVES: 4
$1.97/$0.49 per person

CHERRIES JUBILEE ICE CREAM PARFAIT

1	(12-ounce) bag frozen cherries	$2.49
¼	cup sugar	$0.05
¼	cup orange juice	$0.06
¼	cup brandy, optional	$1.56
1	tbsp. cornstarch	$0.01
2	cups vanilla ice cream	$0.80
16	chocolate cream cookies, broken into pieces	$0.51

In a saucepan over medium heat, combine the cherries, sugar, and orange juice. Bring to a simmer. Add the brandy, if using, and continue simmering until the alcohol burns off, about 2 minutes. In a small bowl, stir together the cornstarch with 2 tablespoons water. Stir the slurry into the cherry mixture and simmer until it thickens, about 1–2 minutes. Let cool.

In parfait glasses, put a small scoop of ice cream, a spoonful or two of the cherry mixture, and some of the cookie pieces. Repeat layering to fill up the glass. Serve immediately.

SERVES: 4
COOK TIME: 10 minutes
$3.92/$0.98 per person

CAJUN QUESADILLA

	Reserved chicken and vegetable mixture, chopped (page 38)	$0.00
4	large flour tortillas	$0.72
1	cup shredded MontereyJack cheese	$1.00
2	tbsp. canola oil	$0.06
	Reserved remoulade	$0.00

Preheat grill pan over medium heat.

In a small skillet over medium-high heat, add the chicken and vegetable mixture and cook until the chicken is cooked through, about 5 minutes.

Brush one side of two tortillas with the oil and put them oil-side down. Spread half the chicken mixture on each tortilla. Sprinkle half the cheese over each, and top with the other tortillas. Brush the tops with oil. Put the quesadillas on the grill pan and cook until the bottom is browned, about 2–3 minutes. Flip them over and cook until the bottom is browned and the cheese is melted, another 2–3 minutes. Slice and serve with the remoulade.

> **MAKES:** 4 half-quesadillas
> **COOK TIME:** 5 minutes
> **$1.78 in extra ingredients**

Please see Main Recipes on pages 36 and 38

CAJUN RED BEAN AND RICE SOUP

4	cups chicken broth	$1.60
1	tsp. Cajun seasoning	$0.11
1	tsp. hot sauce	$0.02
	Reserved rice mixture (page 38)	$0.00
1	(15-ounce) can red kidney beans, drained and rinsed	$0.75
2	sliced scallions	$0.26
	Kosher salt, to taste	$0.00
	Black pepper, to taste	$0.00

In a medium saucepan over medium heat, add the broth, Cajun seasoning, and hot sauce and bring to a simmer. Stir in the rice mixture and beans and cook until hot, about 5 minutes. Taste, and adjust the seasoning with salt and pepper. Serve garnished with scallions.

> **SERVES:** 4
> **COOK TIME:** 10 minutes
> **$2.74 in extra ingredients**

Please see Main Recipe on page 38

5. CHEAPER BY THE DOZEN

- Poach 'em, fry 'em, or scramble 'em. Today's recipes prove that eggs make great meals.
- **Meal total: $14.34/$1.19 per person**
  Savory Bread Pudding with Sausage and Mushrooms, Spinach and Potato Frittata, Farmhouse Hash with Poached Eggs, and Fried Bread Pudding Bites

---

1. Savory Bread Pudding with Sausage and Mushrooms

Total cost: $6.81/$1.14 per person

> **TIP:** *Presliced mushrooms are the same price as whole mushrooms. Just remember the presliced have a shorter shelf life, so make sure you use them right away.*

2. Spinach and Potato Frittata

Total cost: $2.89/$0.72 per person

3. Farmhouse Hash with Poached Eggs

Total cost: $4.00/$1.00 per person

4. R2R: Fried Bread Pudding Bites

$0.64 in extra ingredients

5. R2R: Farmhouse Hash Taquitos

$1.36 in extra ingredients

MSM TIP:

Compare price:
Pork = $2.99/lb
Turkey = $3.99/lb
Chicken = $4.29/lb

SAVORY BREAD PUDDING WITH SAUSAGE AND MUSHROOMS

½	pound sweet Italian sausage, removed from casing	$1.50
1	(8-ounce) package sliced mushrooms	$2.49
1	tbsp. canola oil	$0.03
½	loaf cubed country-style bread	$1.50
4	eggs	$0.68
2	cups milk	$0.48
1	tsp. Italian seasoning	$0.13
½	tsp. kosher salt	$0.00
¼	tsp. black pepper	$0.00

Preheat oven to 325°F. Spray a twelve-count muffin tin with nonstick cooking spray and set aside.

In a large skillet over medium heat, sauté sausage until browned. Remove to a plate and set aside. Add canola oil and mushrooms and sauté until mushrooms are lightly browned. Remove from heat, stir in cooked sausage, and let cool.

In a large bowl, whisk together the eggs, milk, Italian seasoning, salt, and pepper. Add the cubed bread, sausage, and mushroom to the egg mixture. Let the egg and bread mixture sit for at least 30 minutes in the refrigerator to allow the bread to absorb the liquid. Ladle the bread pudding mixture into the muffin tin. Place muffin tin on a sheet tray and pour some hot water into sheet tray. Bake for 35–40 minutes or until set. (Reserve 3 bread puddings for Round 2 Recipe: Fried Bread Pudding Bites, page 50.)

SERVES: 6
COOK TIME: 50 minutes
$6.81/$1.14 per person

Please see Round 2 Recipe on page 50

SPINACH AND POTATO FRITTATA

1	russet potato, peeled and thinly sliced	$0.30
4	tbsp. canola oil, divided use	$0.12
½	medium diced yellow onion	$0.14
2	tsp. chopped garlic	$0.02
1	box (10-ounce) frozen chopped spinach, thawed and water squeezed out	$0.89
½	cup shredded mozzarella cheese	$0.50
4	eggs	$0.68
1	cup milk	$0.24
2	tsp. kosher salt	$0.00
½	tsp. black pepper	$0.00

Preheat oven to 450°F. Place a baking sheet into the oven to preheat.

Place the sliced potato in a bowl with 2 tablespoons canola oil, season with 1 teaspoon salt and ½ teaspoon pepper and toss to coat. Remove baking sheet from oven, spray generously with nonstick cooking spray, and add potato slices, making sure they are all in a single layer. Place in oven and bake for 8 minutes.

In a cast-iron skillet, heat the remaining oil over medium heat. Add onion and sauté for 2 minutes. Add garlic and spinach and sauté for another 2 minutes.

In a large bowl whisk together the eggs, milk, and remaining salt and pepper. Mix in cheese and set aside.

Turn the oven down to 350°F. Remove potatoes from oven and add to skillet. Pour in the egg mixture and gently mix in. Place the skillet in the oven and bake for 30–35 minutes, or until eggs have set.

Remove from oven and let cool for 5 minutes. Serve warm or at room temperature.

SERVES: 4
COOK TIME: 45 minutes
$2.89/$0.72 per person

FARMHOUSE HASH WITH POACHED EGGS

½	pound sweet Italian sausage	$1.50
½	medium diced yellow onion	$0.14
1	pound small diced red potatoes	$0.80
1	carrot, diced	$0.16
2	stalks celery	$0.32
1	tsp. chopped garlic	$0.02
½	tsp. red pepper flakes	$0.04
1	tsp. paprika	$0.26
4	eggs	$0.68
1	tbsp. white vinegar	$0.04
2	tbsp. chopped fresh parsley	$0.04
	Kosher salt, to taste	$0.00
	Black pepper, to taste	$0.00

In a large cast-iron skillet over medium heat, brown the sausage. Remove with slotted spoon and place on a plate lined with a paper towel. Add onions, celery, potatoes, carrots, garlic, red pepper flakes, paprika, and season with salt and pepper. Sauté over medium heat, stirring frequently, until potatoes and carrots are tender, about 12 minutes. Stir in cooked sausage.

Bring a medium pot of water to a simmer. Add the vinegar and 1 teaspoon of salt. When water comes up to a simmer, crack an egg into a ladle and carefully slide it into the simmering water. Quickly repeat with remaining eggs. Using a slotted spoon, carefully corral the white of each egg around its yolk. Poach the eggs until the whites are firm, or to the desired degree of doneness, about 3–5 minutes.

Divide the hash between four plates, reserving 1 cup for Round 2 Recipe: Farmhouse Hash Taquitos, page 51. Top each plate of hash with a poached egg and garnish with fresh parsley. Serve with toasted bread slices.

SERVES: 4
COOK TIME: 12 minutes
$4.00/$1.00 per person

Please see Round 2 Recipe on page 51

FRIED BREAD PUDDING BITES

3	leftover bread puddings	$0.00
1	egg, lightly beaten	$0.17
¼	cup milk	$0.06
¼	cup canola oil	$0.12
¼	cup applesauce	$0.14
3	tbsp. brown mustard	$0.08
2	tbsp. sour cream	$0.07

Heat the oil in a 12-inch skillet over medium-high heat.

In a shallow dish or pie plate, whisk together egg and milk. Slice each bread pudding in half horizontally. Carefully place into the hot oil and fry for 3 minutes per side or until brown and crispy. Remove to a plate lined with a paper towel and season with salt and pepper while hot.

In a small bowl whisk together the applesauce, mustard, and sour cream. Serve on the side with fried bread.

SERVES: 4

COOK TIME: 6 minutes

$0.64 in extra ingredients

Please see Main Recipe on page 46

FARMHOUSE HASH TAQUITOS

1	cup reserved farmhouse hash (page 48)	$0.00
1	tsp. chili seasoning	$0.09
2	tsp. chopped fresh cilantro	$0.26
¾	cup Cheddar cheese	$0.63
8	corn tortillas	$0.32
2	tbsp. canola oil	$0.06

Preheat oven to 400°F. Spray a baking sheet with nonstick cooking spray and set aside.

In a medium bowl, combine leftover hash, seasoning, cilantro, and ½ cup of cheese. Wrap tortillas in a damp paper towel and warm in the microwave until pliable, or wrap in foil and warm in oven for 5 minutes. Place 2 tablespoons of the hash-and-cheese mixture on the lower third of a corn tortilla. Roll the tortilla and place seam-side down onto the prepared baking sheet. Top with remaining cheese and bake in oven for 15–20 minutes.

Serve hot.

SERVES: 4
COOK TIME: 20 minutes
$1.36 in extra ingredients

Please see Main Recipe on page 48

6. THE FAMILY KITCHEN

- **Meal total: $19.95/$4.99 per person**
  Grilled Pork Chops with Peach Salsa,
  Caprese Salad Stuffed Tomatoes, White
  Chocolate-Chip Shortcake with Basil
  Strawberries, and a Watermelon Martini

1. Grilled Pork Chops with Peach Salsa
Total cost: $4.72/$1.18 per person

2. Caprese Salad Stuffed Tomatoes
Total cost: $8.61/$2.15 per person

3. White Chocolate-Chip Shortcake with Basil Strawberries
Total cost: $4.91/$1.23 per person

4. Watermelon Martini
Total cost: $1.41/$0.35 per person

> **TIP:** *Prechopped watermelon costs 75% more than chopping your own.*

5. R2R: Grilled Margherita Pizza
$2.12 in extra ingredients

6. R2R: Orzo Soup with Pork
$2.42 in extra ingredients

MSM TIP:
Jarred peach salsa = $4.49
SL's peach salsa = $1.56
Savings = $2.93 or 65%

MSM TIP:
Grocery-store olive bar = $7.99/lb
Fresh packaged block = $3.99/lb
Savings = $4.00 or 50%

MSM TIP:
Premium white chocolate bar = $1.12
White chocolate chips = $0.40
Savings = $0.72 or 64%

GRILLED PORK CHOPS WITH PEACH SALSA

FOR PEACH SALSA:

2	small diced peaches	$1.08
½	small diced red onion	$0.34
1	tsp. chopped fresh cilantro	$0.01
1	tbsp. lime juice	$0.09
1	tsp. olive oil	$0.04
	Kosher salt, to taste	$0.00
	Black pepper, to taste	$0.00

FOR PORK CHOPS:

5	bone-in pork chops, about 2 pounds	$2.98
2	tbsp. canola oil	$0.06
2	tbsp. chili powder	$0.12

FOR THE SALSA:

In a bowl, add peaches, onion (reserve the other half for Round 2 Recipe: Orzo Soup with Pork, page 64), and cilantro. Pour in the lime juice and olive oil, and season with salt and pepper. Toss everything together and set aside.

FOR THE PORK CHOPS:

Heat a grill pan over medium-high heat. Brush the pork chops with the oil, rub with chili powder, and season with salt and pepper. Grill the chops until cooked through to your liking, about 4–6 minutes per side. (Set 2 chops aside for Round 2 Recipe: Orzo Soup with Pork, page 64.)

Serve the chops with big spoonfuls of the peach salsa.

SERVES: 4
COOK TIME: 10 minutes
$4.72 /$1.18 per person

Please see Round 2 Recipe on page 64

CAPRESE SALAD STUFFED TOMATOES

5	beefsteak tomatoes	**$2.98**
1	(16-ounce) package orzo, cooked according to package instructions	**$1.33**
1	(1-pound) block mozzarella	**$3.99**
2	tbsp. chopped fresh basil	**$0.04**
2	tbsp. olive oil	**$0.24**
1	tbsp. red wine vinegar	**$0.03**
	Kosher salt, to taste	**$0.00**
	Black pepper, to taste	**$0.00**

Cut the tops off 4 tomatoes and hollow out the insides. Dice the pulp and the remaining tomato. Dice ½ cup of mozzarella. (Reserve the rest for the Round 2 Recipe: Grilled Margherita Pizza, page 62.)

In a bowl, combine 2 cups of the orzo (reserve the rest for the Round 2 Recipe: Orzo Soup with Pork, page 64), diced mozzarella, ¼ cup of the chopped tomato (reserve the rest for Round 2 Recipe: Grilled Margherita Pizza, page 62), basil, olive oil, vinegar, and salt and pepper to taste. Divide the mixture among the 4 tomato shells and serve.

SERVES: 4
$8.61/$2.15 per person

Please see Round 2 Recipes on pages 62 and 64

WHITE CHOCOLATE-CHIP SHORTCAKE WITH BASIL STRAWBERRIES

1½	cups baking mix	$0.45
¼	cup plus 3 tbsp. sugar	$0.09
⅓	cup milk	$0.05
2	tbsp. melted unsalted butter	$0.12
¼	cup white chocolate chips	$0.40
1	quart sliced strawberries	$3.00
1	tbsp. chopped fresh basil	$0.02
½	cup heavy cream	$0.56
½	tsp. vanilla	$0.22

Preheat oven to 425°F.

In a bowl, whisk together the baking mix and ¼ cup sugar. Stir in the milk and butter, and fold in the chocolate chips. Pat out the dough on a floured surface, cut into 8 triangles, and place on an ungreased baking sheet. Bake until golden brown, about 8–10 minutes. Remove from the oven and let cool. Add the chopped basil to the strawberries and toss to combine.

With an electric hand mixer, whip the cream with three tablespoons of sugar and vanilla. Split open each shortcake and divide strawberries among them. Dollop on the whipped cream and put on a shortcake top.

SERVES: 4
COOK TIME: 10 minutes
$4.91/$1.23 per person

WATERMELON MARTINI

4	cups watermelon, cut into chunks	$0.80
2	tbsp. fresh lemon juice	$0.25
½	cup sugar	$0.03
½	cup water	
1	bottle sparkling water	$0.33
4	ounces citrus vodka, optional	$2.12

In a small sauce pot combine sugar with ½ cup water. Place over medium heat and bring to a boil. Remove from heat and let cool.

In the bowl of a food processor or in a blender, add the watermelon and puree until smooth. Strain out, and discard the pulp.

In a pitcher, stir together the watermelon juice, lemon juice, and simple syrup. Fill cocktail shaker with ice, add some of the watermelon mixture, and shake. Pour into a chilled martini glass and top with sparkling water. Add vodka, if using.

SERVES: 4
$1.41 /$0.35 per person

GRILLED MARGHERITA PIZZA

3	tbsp. olive oil	$0.36
	Reserved chopped tomato (page 56)	$0.00
1	tbsp. chopped garlic	$0.05
1	(16-ounce) package refrigerated pizza dough	$1.69
	Reserved mozzarella, sliced thin (page 56)	$0.00
4	torn basil leaves	$0.02
	Kosher salt, to taste	$0.00
	Black pepper, to taste	$0.00

In a medium skillet over medium heat, add 1 tablespoon of the oil. When it is hot, add the tomato and garlic. Cook down until slightly thickened and the liquid has evaporated, about 5 minutes. Season with salt and pepper to taste, and set aside.

Heat a grill pan over medium heat. Preheat the broiler.

Spread out the pizza dough into a 12 × 6-inch rectangle. Brush with 1 tablespoon of oil. Transfer the dough to the grill pan and bake, oil-side down, until the dough is set and it starts to brown on the bottom side, about 2 minutes. Flip it over, spread on the tomato sauce, and cover with the mozzarella slices. Drizzle the remaining tablespoon of olive oil on top. Put it under the broiler until the cheese is melted and bubbling, about 1 minute.

Scatter the basil leaves over pizza, cut, and serve.

SERVES: 8
COOK TIME: 5 minutes
$2.12 in extra ingredients

Please see Main Recipe on page 56

ORZO SOUP WITH PORK

	Reserved red onion, sliced (page 54)	$0.00
1	quart chicken broth	$1.60
	Reserved pork chop, diced (page 54)	$0.00
	Reserved orzo	$0.00
2	cups baby spinach	$0.71
1	tbsp. lemon juice	$0.08
	Kosher salt, to taste	$0.00
	Black pepper, to taste	$0.00

In a medium pot over medium heat, add the oil. When it is hot, add the onion and cook until it is softened, about 5 minutes.

Add the chicken broth and bring it to a simmer. Add the pork, orzo, and spinach and simmer until heated through and spinach is wilted, about 2 or 3 minutes.

Add the lemon juice, taste, and adjust the seasoning with salt and pepper. Serve hot.

SERVES: 4
COOK TIME: 20 minutes
$2.42 in extra ingredients

Please see Main Recipe on page 54

7. FIESTA CUISINE CLASSICS

- Savory, spicy Cuban fare at a price that will make you cha-cha-cha.
- Food with big Cuban flavor and *precios mas bajos*—that's Spanish for tiny price tags!
- **Meal #1 total: $17.26/$4.32 per person**

   Arroz Con Pollo, slice of Tres Leches Cake, and a Mojito
- **Meal #2 total: $17.26/$4.21 per person**

   Cuban Sandwiches with Plantain Chips, slice of Tres Leches Cake,

   and a Mojito

---

1. Arroz Con Pollo
   Total cost: $10.26/$2.57 per person

2. Cuban Sandwiches with Plantain Chips
   Total cost: $9.83/$2.46 per person

3. Tres Leches Cake
   Total cost: $5.77/$0.72 per person

4. Cuban Mojito
   Total cost: $1.23/$0.31 per person,

   $0.43 with an ounce of white rum

5. R2R: Rice Cakes with Creamy Cilantro Sauce
   Total cost: $0.97 in extra ingredients

6. R2R: Black Bean and Pork Stew
   Total cost: $2.20 in extra ingredients

MSM TIP:

Buying a whole chicken is the most cost-effective way to keep your chicken dishes money-saving. Store chicken in a plastic bag (just in case there are any leaks in packaging) in your refrigerator for up to 2 days, or freeze until ready to use.

ARROZ CON POLLO

2	tbsp. canola oil	$0.06
1	(4-pound) chicken, cut into 8 pieces	$6.76
1	medium chopped yellow onion (reserve ½ for Round 2 Recipe)	$0.28
1	chopped green bell pepper (reserve ½ for Round 2 Recipe)	$0.89
1	tbsp. chopped garlic	$0.05
1	tbsp. chili powder	$0.06
1	(8-ounce) can tomato sauce	$0.32
¾	cup olives stuffed with pimentos, drained	$0.92
4	cups water	$0.00
3	cups long grain rice	$0.90
1	tbsp. chopped fresh cilantro	$0.02
	Kosher salt, to taste	$0.00
	Black pepper, to taste	$0.00

In a large heavy-bottomed pot over medium-high heat, add the oil. Season the chicken with salt and pepper, and brown in batches on both sides, about 4–5 minutes per side. Remove the chicken to a plate. To the pot add half the onion and half the green pepper. (Reserve half of the onion and green pepper for the Round 2 Recipe: Black Bean and Pork Stew, page 74.)

Cook until softened, about 5 minutes, then add the garlic and chili powder. Stir in the rice and let it toast for 5 minutes.

Add the water, tomato sauce, and olives, and give it a big stir. Put the chicken back into the pot. Bring to a boil, lower the heat, cover, and simmer until the chicken is cooked through and the rice is tender, about 30–35 minutes. (Reserve 2 cups of rice mixture for Round 2 Recipe: Rice Cakes with Creamy Cilantro Sauce, page 73.) Serve garnished with cilantro.

SERVES: 4
COOK TIME: 1 hour
$10.26/$2.57 per person

Please see Round 2 Recipes on pages 73 and 74

CUBAN SANDWICHES WITH PLANTAIN CHIPS

1	(1½-pound) pork rib loin end roast	$2.99
2	tsp. canola oil	$0.01
1	large French baguette	$1.69
¼	cup spicy brown mustard	$0.18
⅓	pound deli ham, thinly sliced	$1.66
¼	pound Swiss cheese, thinly sliced	$1.35
1	large dill pickle, thinly sliced	$0.15
3	tbsp. unsalted butter, softened	$0.18
	Kosher salt, to taste	$0.00
	Black pepper, to taste	$0.00

FOR PLANTAIN CHIPS:

2	large green plantains, peeled and sliced thin	$0.66
2	cups canola oil, for frying	$0.96
	Kosher salt, to taste	$0.00

FOR THE PORK:

Bring the pork to room temperature. Rub it with the oil and season with salt and pepper. Put the roast onto a baking pan and cook until the internal temperature reaches 150°F, about 40–45 minutes.

SERVES: 4

COOK TIME: 55 minutes

$9.83/$2.46 per person

Cover the pork with foil and let it come to room temperature, about 45–60 minutes. When you are ready to make sandwiches, thinly slice about ¾ of the pork roast. (Reserve one quarter of the pork roast for Round 2 Recipe: Black Bean and Pork Stew, page 74.)

TO ASSEMBLE THE SANDWICH:

Heat a grill pan over medium heat. Slice the bread in half horizontally. Spread a thin layer of mustard on both halves of the bread. Place an even layer of ham over the bottom half. Top with the pork, Swiss cheese, and pickles. Put the top on the sandwich and spread a thin layer of butter on the outside of the bread. Put the sandwich on the grill. Set a baking sheet on top of the sandwich, and weigh it down with a heavy skillet. Cook until the bottom is crisp and the cheese is starting to melt, about 4–5 minutes. Flip the sandwich over, replace the weighted baking sheet, and cook another 3–4 minutes. Cut into 4 equal sandwiches, then slice each sandwich diagonally.

FOR THE PLANTAIN CHIPS:

In a 2-inch-deep cast-iron skillet, heat the oil to 350°F. Cook the plantain slices in batches until they are browned and crispy, about 3–4 minutes. Drain on brown paper and season with salt.

Please see Round 2 Recipe on page 74

TIP: *Plantains, which look similar to bananas, can be found in any Mexican market and some major grocery stores. Make sure you buy the green plantains; they are better for slicing and frying, because they are firmer, starchy, and less sweet. Fully ripened plantains will be yellow, brown-spotted, and much sweeter.*

TRES LECHES CAKE

1	(18.25-ounce) box yellow cake mix	$0.99
⅓	cup canola oil	$0.16
3	large eggs	$0.33
1	(14-ounce) can sweetened condensed milk	$1.59
1	(12-ounce) can evaporated milk, divided use	$0.89
1¼	cups heavy cream	$1.40
½	tsp. vanilla	$0.22
½	cup flaked toasted coconut	$0.19

Preheat the oven to 350°F. Spray a 9 × 13-inch cake pan with nonstick spray.

In a large bowl, add the cake mix, 1 cup evaporated milk, oil, and eggs. Using an electric hand mixer on medium speed, combine and beat for 2 minutes. Pour the batter into the prepared pan, and bake until a toothpick inserted in the middle of the cake comes out clean, about 30–35 minutes. Let cool while you combine the milk.

In a medium bowl, whisk together the sweetened condensed milk, remaining evaporated milk, and ¼ cup cream. Using a fork, poke holes all over the cake in the pan. Pour the milk mixture evenly onto the cake and let it cool to room temperature, about 1 hour. Cover and refrigerate until the liquid absorbs into the cake, about 2–3 hours or overnight.

When you are ready to serve, in a large bowl, add the remaining cream and vanilla. Beat with an electric hand mixer on high speed until the cream holds soft peaks. Spread the cream over the cake and sprinkle with the toasted coconut.

SERVES: 12
COOK TIME: 35 minutes
$5.77/$0.72 per person

TIP: *A sweet, rich dessert at an even sweeter price! Tres Leches translates to "three milks," which is what gives this cake its intensely moist, milky texture—a combination of heavy cream, evaporated milk, and sweetened condensed milk. Plan ahead when you want to make this cake, because it requires a long soaking, up to overnight. Worth the wait, Tres Leches Cake is sweet, moist, and light.*

CUBAN MOJITO

16	mint leaves	$0.20
2	chopped limes	$0.66
8	tsp. sugar	$0.04
1	liter sparkling water	$0.33
4	ounces white rum (optional)	$1.72

In four highball glasses, add 4 mint leaves, ½ lime, and 2 teaspoons sugar. Muddle ingredients in the bottom of the glass, using a muddler or a wooden spoon. Add ice to each glass, top with the sparkling water, and stir. Add 1 ounce rum to each glass, if using.

SERVES: 4
$1.23/$0.31 per person

RICE CAKES WITH CREAMY CILANTRO SAUCE

1	cup bread crumbs	$0.56
	Reserved 2 cups rice mixture, chilled (page 68)	$0.00
¼	cup canola oil for frying	$0.12
1	egg	$0.11

FOR CREAMY CILANTRO SAUCE:

½	cup fresh cilantro leaves	$0.16
1	tbsp. red wine vinegar	$0.03
½	tsp. chopped garlic	$0.01
2	tbsp. sour cream	$0.09
	Kosher salt, to taste	$0.00
	Black pepper, to taste	$0.00

Put the bread crumbs onto a plate. Take ¼ cup of the chilled rice mixture and form it into a ½-inch-thick patty. Press the patty into the bread crumbs and set aside while you form the rest and make the sauce.

To make the sauce, in the bowl of a food processor, add the cilantro, vinegar, garlic, and sour cream, and process to combine. Taste, and adjust the seasoning with salt and pepper.

In a nonstick skillet over medium heat, add the oil. When it is hot, fry the rice cakes in batches until they are golden brown and crispy on both sides, about 8–10 minutes. Drain on brown paper.

Serve the rice cakes drizzled with the sauce.

TIP: *These rice cakes can be served as an appetizer, alongside a salad for dinner, or even as a quick snack for kids after school. Rice cakes are a great way to serve up any leftover rice you have. Once you get the method down, you can incorporate other flavors and ingredients, depending on what you have lying around!*

SERVES: 4
COOK TIME: 10 minutes
$0.97 in extra ingredients

Please see Main Recipe on page 68

BLACK BEAN AND PORK STEW

1	tbsp. canola oil	$0.03
	Reserved chopped yellow onion, (page 68)	$0.00
	Reserved chopped green bell pepper (page 68)	$0.00
1	tsp. chopped garlic	$0.01
1	tsp. chili powder	$0.02
2	(15-ounce) cans black beans, drained and rinsed	$1.34
2	cups chicken broth	$0.80
	Reserved chopped pork (page 69)	$0.00

In a medium pot over medium heat, add the oil. When it is hot, add the onion and pepper and cook until they begin to soften, about 5 minutes. Add the garlic and chili powder, and cook for 30 seconds. Add the beans and broth and bring to a simmer. Cook for 10 minutes. Using a potato masher, mash some of the black beans to thicken the stew. Add the pork and heat through.

SERVES: 4

COOK TIME: 20 minutes

$2.20 in extra ingredients

Please see Main Recipes on pages 68 and 69

8. FARM STAND FRESH

- **Meal #1 total: $18.35/$4.59 per person**

   Portobello Burgers, Zucchini Cakes, Strawberry Orange Daiquiri, and Berry Custard Pie

- **Meal #2 total: $16.96/$4.24 per person**

   Veggie Lasagna, Strawberry Orange Daiquiri, and Berry Custard Pie

1. Portobello Burgers

Total cost: **$7.17/$1.79 per person**

2. Zucchini Cakes

Total cost: **$3.54/$0.89 per person**

3. Veggie Lasagna

Total cost: **$9.32/$2.33 per person**

> **TIP:** Use walnuts in my pesto instead of traditional pine nuts; the flavor is a little different but still delicious.

4. Strawberry Orange Daiquiri

Total cost: **$2.10/$0.53 per person**

5. Berry Custard Pie

Total cost: **$5.54/$0.69 per person**

> **MSM TIP:**
> Per pound, pine nuts cost $1.17, vs. walnuts at $0.84. You'll save $0.33 or 28%.

> It is faster to buy a premade piecrust, but in the case of graham cracker crust . . . it is also cheaper! Blueberries and raspberries are cheapest in the summer months, which is also when they are at their best. If you want to make this pie over the winter months, using frozen berries will keep the cost down.

6. R2R: Stuffed Zucchini Boats

Total cost: **$0.78 in extra ingredients**

7. R2R: Eggplant Rollatini

Total cost: **$2.72 in extra ingredients**

PORTOBELLO BURGERS

4	portobello mushrooms	$3.99
2	tbsp. canola oil	$0.06
2	tbsp. red wine vinegar	$0.05
2	tsp. Worcestershire sauce	$0.03
1	tbsp. finely chopped garlic	$0.20
2	tsp. grill seasoning	$0.16
¼	pound Cheddar cheese	$1.00
1	sliced tomato	$0.48
4	leaves romaine lettuce	$0.30
4	hamburger buns	$0.64
	Kosher salt, to taste	$0.00
	Black pepper, to taste	$0.00

AIOLI SAUCE

2	tbsp. reserved marinade	
¼	cup mayonnaise	$0.26

Rub mushroom caps with a damp cloth to clean. Remove stems (reserve for Round 2 Recipe: Stuffed Zucchini Boats, page 86).

In a pie plate or shallow baking dish, combine the oil, vinegar, Worcestershire sauce, garlic, grill seasoning, and salt and pepper to taste. (Reserve 2 tablespoons of the marinade for the aioli.) Add mushroom caps, turning to coat completely with marinade. Let sit at room temperature for 15 minutes, flipping after 7 minutes.

Heat a grill pan or outdoor grill on medium heat. Grill mushroom caps about 5 minutes on each side. Two minutes before they are done, top with cheese. While mushrooms are grilling, make aioli sauce by combining 2 tablespoons of the marinade with ¼ cup mayonnaise. Toast hamburger buns and spread each half with aioli sauce.

Remove mushrooms from grill and serve on toasted buns with lettuce and tomato slices.

TIP: *Portobello mushrooms are a great substitute for beef in burgers. They are meaty and dense in texture and, best of all, they are really good for you!*

SERVES: 4
COOK TIME: 35 minutes
$7.17/$1.79 per person

Please see Round 2 Recipe on page 86

ZUCCHINI CAKES

3	zucchini	$2.50
½	medium yellow onion, diced small	$0.14
1	tbsp. minced garlic	$0.07
1	cup Bisquick baking mix	$0.30
2	eggs, lightly beaten	$0.22
¼	cup canola oil	$0.12
½	cup sour cream, for serving	$0.19
	Kosher salt, to taste	$0.00
	Black pepper, to taste	$0.00

Grate 1 zucchini (reserve 2 for Round 2 Recipe: Stuffed Zucchini Boats, page 86). Place grated zucchini in a clean kitchen towel and squeeze well to remove moisture.

In a large bowl, combine all ingredients except the canola oil and sour cream. Mix well to thoroughly combine.

Heat canola oil in a heavy skillet over medium heat. Drop zucchini mixture into skillet in ¼-cup measures. Fry on both sides until golden brown and cooked through, about 3 minutes per side. Remove from pan and drain on a paper-lined sheet pan.

In a small bowl, mix together sour cream with parsley, salt, and pepper. Serve zucchini cakes topped with a dollop of parsley sour cream.

SERVES: 4
COOK TIME: 15 minutes
$3.54/$0.89 per person

Please see Round 2 Recipe on page 86

VEGGIE LASAGNA

2	large eggplants	$2.08
1	yellow squash	$0.73
¼	cup canola oil	$0.09
2	tbsp. balsamic vinegar	$0.19
2	green bell peppers, roasted, peeled, and seeded	$0.96
3	cups ricotta cheese	$2.64
1	egg, beaten	$0.11
½	cup grated mozzarella cheese	$0.50
1	tbsp. chopped fresh oregano	$0.02
2	tbsp. chopped fresh parsley	$0.04
	Kosher salt, to taste	$0.00
	Black pepper, to taste	$0.00

BASIL WALNUT PESTO:

1	cup fresh basil	$0.32
1	tbsp. minced garlic	$0.07
¼	cup chopped walnuts	$0.84
¼	cup Parmesan cheese	$0.58
⅓	cup olive oil	$0.15

SERVES: 4
COOK TIME: 45 minutes
$9.32/$2.33 per person

Preheat a grill pan over medium-high heat, and preheat the oven to 350°F.

Slice eggplant and squash lengthwise into ½-inch strips. Place in a large bowl and drizzle canola oil and balsamic vinegar over top. Toss with salt and pepper. Place on hot grill and cook about 2 minutes on each side. (Reserve 6 pieces of grilled eggplant for Round 2 Recipe: Eggplant Rollatini, page 87.)

In a small bowl, combine the ricotta with egg, oregano, parsley, salt, and pepper.

In a 9 × 9-inch baking dish, put down a single layer of grilled eggplant and top with a single layer of bell peppers. Spread ⅓ of ricotta mixture over top. Layer another single layer of eggplant, followed by one of grilled squash. Top with another ⅓ of the ricotta mixture (save remainder of ricotta mixture for Round 2 Recipe: Eggplant Rollatini, page 87) and a final layer of eggplant and any remaining roasted peppers and yellow squash. Sprinkle with mozzarella cheese. Cover with aluminum foil and bake for 30–35 minutes or until heated through and cheese is bubbling. Remove from oven and allow to cool for 10 minutes.

TO MAKE BASIL WALNUT PESTO:

In the bowl of a food processor, pulse together the basil, garlic, walnuts, and Parmesan cheese. With food processor running, slowly drizzle in olive oil. Season with salt and pepper.

Cut lasagna into 4 squares and serve topped with a generous spoonful of pesto.

Please see Round 2 Recipe on page 87

STRAWBERRY ORANGE DAIQUIRI

1	pint fresh strawberries	$2.00
1	orange	$0.06
¼	cup sugar	$0.04
¼	cup water	$0.00
6	ounces rum, optional	$3.75

Using a vegetable peeler, remove the outside of orange, taking care to leave the pith behind.

In a small saucepan over medium heat, whisk together the sugar, water, and orange zest. Bring to a simmer and remove from heat. Cool to room temperature.

Juice the orange in a blender. Reserve 4 strawberries for garnish; remove the hulls and rough-chop the remainder. Add the strawberries to the blender and puree. Fill blender with ice. Add the cooled orange simple syrup, and the rum, if using, and crush ice to smooth consistency.

SERVES: 4
$2.10/$0.53 per person

BERRY CUSTARD PIE

1	(9-inch) graham cracker crust	$1.49
3	eggs	$0.33
½	cup sugar	$0.10
1½	cups milk	$0.24
2	tsp. vanilla	$0.88
½	cup blueberries	$1.25
½	cup raspberries	$1.25
	Pinch of kosher salt	$0.00

Preheat oven to 350°F.

In a medium bowl, beat together the eggs with sugar and salt until pale. Slowly beat in the milk and vanilla.

Cover bottom of piecrust with the berries. Pour egg mixture over top, bake for 40–45 minutes or until knife inserted near the center comes out clean (center will be slightly loose). Remove from oven and cool to room temperature before serving.

SERVES: 8
COOK TIME: 45 minutes
$5.54/$0.69 per person

STUFFED ZUCCHINI BOATS

	Reserved 2 zucchini (page 80)	**$0.00**
	Reserved portobello	**$0.00**
	mushroom stems (page 78)	
⅓	cup fresh bread crumbs	**$0.06**
¼	cup shredded	**$0.25**
	mozzarella cheese	
¼	cup chopped Spanish olives	**$0.30**
1	egg, beaten	**$0.11**
1	tsp. Italian seasoning	**$0.06**
	Kosher salt, to taste	**$0.00**
	Black pepper, to taste	**$0.00**

Preheat oven to 350°F.

Slice zucchini lengthwise and scoop out seeds from the center with a spoon.

In a medium bowl, combine the remaining ingredients. Fill the centers of each zucchini half with the mixture.

Place on a nonstick baking sheet and bake for about 20 minutes, until cheese is melted and filling is golden brown and toasted. Serve hot or at room temperature.

SERVES: 4
COOK TIME: 20 minutes
$0.78 in extra ingredients

Please see Main Recipes on pages 78 and 80

EGGPLANT ROLLATINI

	Reserved grilled eggplant (page 82)	$0.00
	Reserved ricotta mixture (page 82)	$0.00
½	cup shredded mozzarella cheese	$1.00
2	tbsp. olive oil	$0.24
2	tsp. garlic, minced	$0.03
½	medium chopped yellow onion	$0.14
1	(28-ounce) can crushed tomatoes	$1.29
1	tbsp. chopped fresh basil	$0.02

Preheat oven to 350°F.

In a medium saucepan over medium-high heat, sauté the onions until softened, about 3 minutes. Add the garlic and cook for another minute. Add the crushed tomatoes and bring to a simmer. Allow to cook for 20 minutes. Remove from heat and stir in the chopped basil.

In a medium bowl, stir the ricotta mixture together with the mozzarella cheese.

Lay out grilled eggplant strips and place about 2 tablespoons of filling onto the bottom of each. Roll up from bottom.

Spread 1 cup of the tomato sauce onto the bottom of a small baking dish. Place eggplant rolls seam-side down into the baking dish. Cover rolls completely with another cup of sauce and bake in oven for 25–35 minutes or until cheese is melted and bubbly.

SERVES: 4
COOK TIME: 55 minutes
$2.72 in extra ingredients

Please see Main Recipe on page 82

9. FEEDING A CROWD

- Entertain on a budget and cook for a crowd on pennies—this crowd-pleaser feeds ten people!
- **Menu Total: $25.27/$2.52 per person**
  Slow-cooked Orange Pork-Shoulder Tacos with Cabbage Slaw, Grilled Corn and Bean Salsa with Oven-Baked Corn Chips, and Coconut Flan with Crispy Coconut Cookies

1. Slow-cooked Orange Pork-Shoulder Tacos with Cabbage Slaw
Total cost: $15.00/$1.50 per person

> *Total cost for Tacos: $12.11/$1.21 per person, $0.60 a taco*
>
> *Total cost for Cabbage Slaw: $2.89/$0.29 per person*

2. Grilled Corn and Bean Salsa with Oven-Baked Corn Chips
Total cost: $4.29/$0.43 per person

3. Coconut Flan with Crispy Coconut Cookies
Total cost: $5.98/$0.60 per person

> *Make coconut flan from scratch. It costs a bit more than the box mix, but the flavor in this quick-scratch recipe makes it well worth the extra pennies.*

4. R2R: Pulled Pork Sliders
$6.96 in extra ingredients

5. R2R: Pork Nachos
$1.12 in extra ingredients

MSM TIP:
Compare price of onions
Chop your own = $0.28
Frozen chopped = $0.56
Savings = $0.28 or 50%

MSM TIP:
Chop your own garlic, because it costs you 5 cents for the amount you need. Store-bought prechopped would be 10 cents. Every penny counts!

MSM TIP:
Baking your own chips costs 65 cents, whereas a store-bought bag is $2.50, so you save $1.85. Compare that to almost $10 for store-bought chips and salsa, and you save more than $5.00.

MSM TIP:
Compare price of tomatoes
Canned diced = $0.99
Canned whole = $0.99
Fresh = $3.12
Savings = $2.13 or 68%

SLOW-COOKED ORANGE PORK-SHOULDER TACOS WITH CABBAGE SLAW

1	medium chopped yellow onion	$0.28
1	(10-pound) bone-in pork shoulder	$9.99
1	tbsp. chopped garlic	$0.05
2	tbsp. soy sauce	$0.11
1	cup orange marmalade	$0.88
20	corn tortillas	$0.80
	Kosher salt, to taste	$0.00
	Black pepper, to taste	$0.00

RED CABBAGE SLAW:

1	small head red cabbage	$2.13
4	medium coarsely grated carrots	$0.64
¼	cup cider vinegar	$0.12
1	tsp. kosher salt	$0.00
	Black pepper, to taste	$0.00

Place the onions in the bottom of a 5-quart slow cooker. Season the pork roast with salt and pepper. Stir together garlic and soy sauce and rub all over pork roast. Place the roast in the slow cooker and spoon marmalade over the top. Cover and cook on low for 8 hours.

When meat is done, remove from slow cooker, let rest for 5 minutes, then shred or break up with a fork and arrange on a platter. Strain sauce and stir 1 cup into shredded pork.

Warm tortillas slightly in a 250°F oven. Set out pork and tortillas with red cabbage slaw, and have guests assemble their own tacos.

Use leftovers from this recipe to make Pulled Pork Sliders with Mustard BBQ Sauce and Pickled Onions (page 96).

TO MAKE CABBAGE SLAW:

Finely shred cabbage with a sharp knife. Mix vinegar, salt, and pepper in a large bowl. Add cabbage and carrots and toss to combine. Use as topping for pulled-pork tacos.

SERVES: 10
COOK TIME: 8 hours
$12.11/$1.21 per person

SERVES: 10
$2.89/$0.29 per person

Please see Round 2 Recipe on page 96

GRILLED CORN AND BEAN SALSA WITH OVEN-BAKED CORN CHIPS

FOR SALSA:

4	shucked ears corn (fresh in season)	**$1.00**
1	tbsp. vegetable oil	**$0.03**
1	tsp. chili powder	**$0.03**
1	(28-ounce) can diced tomatoes, well drained	**$0.99**
1	(15-ounce) can black beans, drained and rinsed	**$0.67**
½	medium diced red onion	**$0.34**
1	minced jalapeño pepper	**$0.29**
1	tsp. chopped garlic	**$0.02**
2	tbsp. lime juice	**$0.17**
¼	cup chopped fresh cilantro	**$0.10**
	Kosher salt, to taste	**$0.00**
	Black pepper, to taste	**$0.00**

Set up grill for direct cooking over medium heat.

Brush corn with oil and season with chili powder and pepper. Place on hot grill and cook about 10 minutes, turning frequently. Remove and let cool. When cool enough to handle, cut kernels from the cob. Place corn in a bowl with tomatoes, beans, onion, and jalapeño pepper. Whisk together lime juice, garlic, and cilantro. Pour over vegetables and beans and toss to combine. Season with salt and pepper. (Reserve 1 cup salsa for Round 2 Recipe: Pork Nachos, p. 98.)

OPTIONAL INDOOR ROASTED CORN:

Preheat oven to 400°F. Cut corn kernels from cob and place on baking sheet. Drizzle with oil, chili powder, salt, and pepper. Roast in oven for about 10 minutes. Remove and let cool. Assemble salad as previously directed.

SERVES: 10

COOK TIME: 20 minutes

SALSA: $4.29/$0.43 per person

CORN CHIPS: $0.65/$0.07 per person

Please see Round 2 Recipe on page 98

OVEN-BAKED CORN CHIPS

15	corn tortillas	$0.60
	Canola oil spray	$0.05
	Kosher salt	$0.00

Preheat oven to 400°F.

Cut each tortilla into 8 triangular portions. Arrange in a single layer on a sheet pan. Spray with canola oil cooking spray, sprinkle with salt, and bake until crisp and lightly browned, about 10 minutes. Allow to cool, and serve with salsa. (Reserve corn chips for Round 2 Recipe: Pork Nachos, p. 98.)

COCONUT FLAN WITH CRISPY COCONUT COOKIES

FOR FLAN:

½	cup plus ⅔ cup sugar, divided	**$0.25**
2	tbsp. water	**$0.00**
6	eggs	**$1.02**
2	egg yolks, reserve whites for cookies	**$0.34**
2	(14-ounce) cans coconut milk	**$2.58**
2	tsp. vanilla	**$0.84**
¼	tsp. kosher salt	**$0.00**

FOR COOKIES:

4	tbsp. melted butter	**$0.24**
2	reserved egg whites, lightly beaten	**$0.00**
½	cup sugar	**$0.11**
½	cup flour	**$0.08**
¼	cup sweetened shredded coconut	**$0.50**

FOR THE FLAN:

Preheat oven to 325°F.

In a small saucepan combine the ½ cup sugar with 2 tablespoons water and heat until the sugar is completely dissolved and it turns a golden brown color.

Carefully pour the caramelized sugar into the bottom of a 10-inch cake pan. Tilt the pan from side to side in a circular motion, swirling the sugar around so that it evenly coats the bottom of the pan. Place the cake pan into a baking dish large enough to accommodate the cake pan and set aside to cool. The sugar will harden as it cools.

In a large mixing bowl, beat eggs and egg yolks slightly; add the ⅔ cup sugar and salt and whisk in the coconut milk and vanilla. Pour custard mixture over the caramelized sugar. Bake at 325°F for 1 hour or until knife inserted near center comes out clean. Cool to room temperature, then chill overnight. To unmold, run a knife around the edge of the baking dish and invert onto a plate.

SERVES: 10
COOK TIME: 40 minutes
$5.98/$0.60 per person

FOR THE COOKIES:

Preheat oven to 400°F and line 2 baking sheets with parchment paper.

In a medium bowl, sift together the flour, sugar, and salt. Beat in the melted butter and egg whites until well incorporated.

Drop batter by tablespoons onto parchment-lined baking sheet. Using an offset spatula, spread cookies to 4-inch circles about ¼ inch thick. Sprinkle with coconut and bake 6–7 minutes or until slightly browned. Allow to cool completely on the baking sheet. Carefully peel from parchment and serve with coconut flan.

TIP: *In this recipe, coconut is a great substitute for heavy cream, because it adds flavor and keeps the flan rich and creamy. You can use milk, but the flan will be less rich and creamy.*

PULLED PORK SLIDERS WITH MUSTARD BBQ SAUCE AND PICKLED ONIONS

PICKLED RED ONION:

1	medium thinly sliced red onion	$0.67
½	tsp. garlic	$0.02
1	jalapeño pepper, cored, seeded, and julienned	$0.29
¼	cup sugar	$0.06
¾	cup cider vinegar	$0.36
1	tsp. kosher salt	$0.00
½	tsp. black pepper	$0.00

MUSTARD BBQ SAUCE:

¼	cup yellow mustard	$0.10
2	tbsp. minced garlic	$0.10
¼	cup cider vinegar (store brand)	$0.12
1	cup barbecue sauce	$0.56

SLIDERS:

	Reserved 3 cups of braised pork shoulder (page 90)	$0.00
12	mini hamburger buns or dinner rolls sliced in half	$3.84 or $4.08

SERVES: 4

COOK TIME: 10 minutes

$6.96 in extra ingredients

FOR THE ONION:

In a medium pot, combine all ingredients except onions with ¾ cup water. Bring to a boil, add the onions, and remove from heat. Let sit until cooled, about 1 hour. Serve with sliders.

FOR THE MUSTARD BBQ SAUCE:

In a small saucepan over medium heat, whisk all the ingredients together. Cook for 5 minutes and remove from heat.

FOR THE SLIDERS:

Place a heaping tablespoon of pulled pork on the bottom halves of the rolls. Drizzle with the barbecue sauce, top with some of the pickled red onions, and place the remaining roll halves on top.

Please see Main Recipe on page 90

PORK NACHOS

	Reserved 2 cups baked corn chips (page 93)	$0.00
	Reserved 1 cup slow-cooked orange pulled pork (page 90)	$0.00
	Reserved 1 cup corn and black bean salsa (page 92)	$0.00
1	cup shredded Cheddar cheese	$0.84
½	cup sour cream, optional	$0.28

Preheat oven to 350°F.

In an ovenproof baking dish, put down a single layer of corn chips. Cover with a layer of the pork, salsa, and cheese. Continue layering, ending with cheese on top. Bake for 10–15 minutes or until cheese is melted and bubbling. Top with sour cream and serve hot.

SERVES: 4
COOK TIME: 15 minutes
$1.12 in extra ingredients

Please see Main Recipes on pages 90, 92, and 93

10. GERMAN FAMILY-FEST

- A culinary tour of Germany! At its heart, German food is hearty, delicious, and very simple, which is why it works great for Money Saving Meals.
- **Meal total: $15.26/$3.81 per person**

  Chicken Schnitzel with Mushroom Sauce, Parsley Dumplings, Frosty Sparkling Apple Cider, and Pear Strudel

---

1. Chicken Schnitzel with Mushroom Sauce
Total cost: $6.68/$1.67 per person

2. Parsley Dumplings
Total cost: $1.26/$0.32 per person

3. Frosty Sparkling Apple Cider
Total cost: $2.01/$0.50 per glass

> *If you want to turn this mocktail into a cocktail, add an ounce of spiced rum for another $0.40 per cocktail, cheers!*

4. Pear Strudel
Total cost: $5.31/$1.33 per person

5. R2R: Cabbage and Pear Slaw
$0.83 in extra ingredients

6. R2R: German Dumpling Soup
$3.65 in extra ingredients

CHICKEN SCHNITZEL WITH MUSHROOM SAUCE

2	bone-in chicken breasts	$2.99
¾	cup flour	$0.11
1	large egg, beaten	$0.11
1	cup plain bread crumbs	$0.56
2	tbsp. chopped fresh parsley	$0.04
¼	cup canola oil	$0.12
2	tbsp. unsalted butter	$0.12
1	(8-ounce) package sliced mushrooms	$1.99
1	tsp. chopped garlic	$0.05
1	cup chicken broth	$0.40
1	tbsp. Worcestershire sauce	$0.06
⅓	cup sour cream	$0.13
	Kosher salt, to taste	$0.00
	Black pepper, to taste	$0.00

Remove the chicken breasts from the bone. Slice each breast horizontally into two pieces. Put them between pieces of plastic wrap and pound them with a mallet or a small skillet until they are ¼ inch thick.

Set up a breading station with three pie plates or shallow dishes. Put the flour in one, the egg beaten with 2 tablespoons of water in the second, and the bread crumbs mixed with 1 tablespoon parsley in the third. Season each piece of chicken with salt and pepper. Dredge the chicken pieces in the flour, then the egg wash, then the bread crumbs. Set aside. In a large skillet over medium heat, add the oil. When the oil is hot, add the chicken in 1 layer and cook until it is golden brown and crispy, about 4–5 minutes per side. Drain on brown paper and keep warm while you make the sauce.

In another skillet over medium heat, add the butter. When it is melted, add mushrooms and season with salt and pepper. Cook until they are browned and the liquid is absorbed, about 6 minutes. Add the garlic and broth and simmer for 2 minutes. Turn the heat off, add the Worcestershire sauce, and stir in the sour cream. Serve the schnitzel with the sauce poured over the top, garnished with the remaining parsley.

TIP: *Each step of the breading process is important. The flour dries the meat, allowing the entire crust to stick to the chicken, and the egg creates some moisture and also makes sure that the bread crumbs stick, creating that crispy, crunchy crust.*

SERVES: 4
COOK TIME: 20 minutes
$6.68/ $1.67 per person

PARSLEY DUMPLINGS (SPAETZLE)

4	cups all-purpose flour	$0.56
4	large eggs	$0.44
¼	cup chopped fresh parsley	$0.08
3	tbsp. unsalted butter	$0.18
2	tsp. kosher salt, plus more to taste	$0.00
	Black pepper, to taste	$0.00

Bring a large pot of water to a boil.

In a large bowl, whisk together the flour, salt, and parsley. In another bowl, whisk together the eggs and ½ cup water. Pour the liquid into the center of the flour mixture. Mix with a wooden spoon until a dough forms, and let rest for 15 minutes.

Using a large sieve or a slotted spoon, form small rustic dumplings by pressing the dough through the holes while holding it over the boiling water. Cook in batches, boiling just until they float, about 1–2 minutes, and drain. (Reserve 2 cups of dumplings for Round 2 Recipe: German Dumpling Soup, page 109.)

In a large skillet over medium-high heat, add the butter. When it is melted, add a layer of spaetzle (dumplings) to the skillet, and cook until they are golden and slightly crispy in places, about 5 minutes. Season with salt and pepper and serve immediately.

SERVES: 4
COOK TIME: 7 minutes
$1.26/$0.32 per person

Please see Round 2 Recipe on page 109

FROSTY SPARKLING APPLE CIDER

1	quart apple cider	**$1.28**
1	cup white cranberry juice	**$0.40**
1	liter bottle sparkling water	**$0.33**
4	ounces spiced rum, optional	**$1.72**

Put 4 mugs in the freezer for at least 30 minutes to chill.

In a pitcher, stir together 3¼ cups apple cider and the cranberry juice. (Reserve the remaining cider for Round 2 Recipes: Cabbage and Pear Slaw, page 108; German Dumpling Soup, page 109.) Pour into the chilled mugs and top with sparkling water.

For the adults, add 1 ounce spiced rum to each drink.

SERVES: 4
$2.01/$0.50 per person

Please see Round 2 Recipe on this pages 108 and 109

PEAR STRUDEL

2	tbsp. unsalted butter	$0.12
4	pears, peeled, cored, and chopped, about 4 cups (reserve 1 cup for Round 2 Recipe, page 108)	$1.00
¼	cup brown sugar	$0.09
1½	tsp. pumpkin pie spice	$0.45
1	(11-ounce) box piecrust mix	$2.39
2	tbsp. all-purpose flour, for rolling	$0.02
1	large egg, beaten	$0.11
1	tbsp. sugar	$0.01
1	cup heavy cream	$1.12
½	cup apple cider	$0.11

SERVES: 4
COOK TIME: 30 minutes
$5.31/$1.33 per person

Preheat the oven to 400°F.

In a large skillet over medium heat, add the butter. When it is melted, add 3 cups pears (reserve 1 cup for Round 2 Recipe: Cabbage and Pear Slaw, page 108), brown sugar, and 1 teaspoon pumpkin pie spice. Cook until the pears are soft and the liquid thickens, about 5–6 minutes. Let cool.

In a large bowl, combine the piecrust mix and ½ cup cold apple cider, until it forms a ball. Wrap in plastic wrap and chill one hour in the refrigerator. On a floured surface, roll out the dough into a 12 × 10-inch rectangle. Spread the pear mixture in the middle of the rectangle, fold in the short ends, and roll the crust over, enclosing the pear mixture. Place the strudel, seam-side down, onto a baking sheet. In a small bowl, mix together the remaining ½ teaspoon pumpkin pie spice and sugar. Brush the strudel with the egg wash and sprinkle with half the spiced sugar. Make four or five small slits on top to let the steam escape. Bake until golden brown, about 25–30 minutes. Let cool.

When you are ready to serve, whip the cream with the remaining spiced sugar. Serve the strudel topped with whipped cream.

TIP: *Strudel can be made with any fruit, so depending on what you have on hand or what's in season, this is an easy go-to dessert.*

Please see Round 2 Recipe on page 108

CABBAGE AND PEAR SLAW

2	tbsp. canola oil	$0.06
2	tbsp. apple cider vinegar	$0.06
	Reserved 2 tbsp. apple cider (page 105)	$0.00
1	tsp. brown sugar	$0.02
	Reserved pear (page 106)	$0.00
	Reserved ½ head shredded green cabbage (page 109)	$0.00
1	medium sliced red onion	$0.67
1	tbsp. chopped fresh parsley	$0.02
	Kosher salt, to taste	$0.00
	Black pepper, to taste	$0.00

In a large bowl, whisk together the oil, vinegar, cider, sugar, and salt and pepper, to taste. Add the pear, cabbage, onion, and parsley. Toss everything together, taste, and adjust seasoning with salt and pepper.

SERVES: 4

$0.83 in extra ingredients

Please see Main Recipes on pages 105 and 106

GERMAN DUMPLING SOUP

1	tbsp. canola oil	$0.03
1	medium sliced yellow onion	$0.28
1	head shredded green cabbage (reserve half for Round 2 Recipe, page 108)	$1.74
1	quart chicken broth	$1.60
½	cup reserved apple cider (page 105)	$0.00
	Reserved spaetzle (page 104)	$0.00
	Kosher salt, to taste	$0.00
	Black pepper, to taste	$0.00

In a medium pot over medium heat, add the oil. When it is hot, add the onion and cook until it begins to soften, 2–3 minutes. Add the cabbage, season with salt and pepper, and cook until the cabbage begins to soften, about 3–4 minutes.

Add the chicken broth and cider, bring to a boil, reduce to a simmer, and cook until the cabbage and onions are soft, about 8–10 minutes.

Add the spaetzle and heat through. Taste and adjust seasoning with salt and pepper.

TIP: *German dumplings are made from a simple dough and pushed through a perforated pan. It's almost like the German version of gnocchi. And it's incredibly cheap, as you need only flour, water, and eggs—items you usually have on hand anyway. A great last-minute addition to a main dish, dumplings cook quickly and are delicious.*

SERVES: 4
COOK TIME: 15 minutes
$3.65 in extra ingredients

Please see Main Recipes on pages 104 and 105

11. GRILLING ON A STICK

- Fire up your grill and soak those skewers to grill up some tasty treats and serve them on a stick!
- **Meal #1 total: $16.26/$4.06 per person**
    Sausage and Pepper Skewers with Grilled Polenta, Put a Stick in It Cocktail, and Grilled Fruit Skewers with Sweet Yogurt Sauce dessert
- **Meal #2 total: $17.71/$4.43 per person**
    Chicken Satay with Grilled Vegetable Couscous, Put a Stick in It Cocktail, and Grilled Fruit Skewers with Sweet Yogurt Sauce dessert

1. Sausage and Pepper Skewers with Grilled Polenta
Total cost: $9.85/$2.46 per person

Green peppers are always going to be cheaper than red peppers, because red peppers have to stay on the vine longer to get that red color

2. Chicken Satay with Grilled Vegetable Couscous
Total cost: $11.30/$2.83 per person

3. Grilled Fruit Skewers with Sweet Yogurt Sauce
Total cost: $5.46/$1.37 per person

4. Put a Stick in It Cocktail
Total cost: $0.95/$0.24 per person

5. R2R: Sausage and Pepper Baked Ziti
$3.17 in extra ingredients

6. R2R: Spicy and Sweet Chicken Wraps
$1.45 in extra ingredients

MSM TIP:
Boneless skinless chicken = $4.99/lb
Thighs = $2.79/lb
Savings = $2.20/lb or 40%

SAUSAGE AND PEPPER SKEWERS WITH GRILLED POLENTA

1	(10-ounce) package quick-cooking polenta	$1.99
5	tbsp. canola oil, for brushing	$0.15
2	pounds hot or sweet Italian sausage	$4.78
1	red bell pepper	$1.24
2	green bell peppers	$0.96
1	large yellow onion	$0.56
1	tsp. Italian seasoning	$0.06
1	tbsp. balsamic vinegar	$0.10
1	tsp. spicy brown mustard	$0.01
	Kosher salt, to taste	$0.00
	Black pepper, to taste	$0.00

Make the polenta according to package directions. Pour the cooked polenta into a greased 9 × 13-inch baking pan and smooth the top. Chill in refrigerator. When the polenta is cold and you are ready to grill, slice it into squares. Brush the squares with a little oil and grill on both sides until they are warmed through and have nice grill marks. Meanwhile, if you are using wooden skewers, soak them in water for at least 30 minutes, or while you prepare the sausage and peppers.

Preheat a grill or grill pan over medium heat. Place the sausages on the grill and cook for 8 minutes, giving them a quarter turn every 2–3 minutes. Remove from grill and let rest for 5 minutes. Cut sausages into 2-inch pieces. They will finish cooking on the skewers with the peppers and onions.

While sausage is cooking, slice the peppers and onion into 2-inch chunks. In a small bowl, whisk together 3 tablespoons canola oil, balsamic vinegar, Italian seasoning, and mustard.

When you are ready, heat your grill or grill pan over medium heat. Drain the skewers and thread them with 3 pieces each of the sausage, onion, and peppers, doubling up the green pepper. Brush them with vinegar mixture and season with salt and pepper. Grill the sausage and peppers on both sides, until they are hot and sizzling. (Reserve 2 skewers for Round 2 Recipe: Sausage and Pepper Baked Ziti, page 118.) Serve with the grilled polenta.

SERVES: 4
COOK TIME: 40 minutes
$9.85/$2.46 per person

Please see Round 2 Recipe on page 118

CHICKEN SATAY WITH GRILLED VEGETABLE COUSCOUS

1	(14-ounce) can unsweetened coconut milk	$1.49
¼	cup brown sugar	$0.09
2	tbsp. soy sauce	$0.18
2	tsp. chopped garlic	$0.04
1	tsp. ground cumin	$0.11
	Zest of ½ orange (reserved from Grilled Fruit Skewers, page 116)	$0.00
2	pounds boneless, skinless chicken thighs	$5.58
½	cup peanut butter	$0.22
1	tbsp. hot sauce, or to taste	$0.06
1	green bell pepper	$0.48
1	medium zucchini	$0.62
1	medium red onion	$0.68
	Canola oil, for brushing	$0.06
1	(10-ounce) package couscous	$1.69
	Kosher salt, to taste	$0.00
	Black pepper, to taste	$0.00

SERVES: 4
COOK TIME: 20 minutes
$11.30/$2.83 per person

In a large bowl, combine the coconut milk, brown sugar, soy sauce, garlic, cumin, orange zest, salt, and pepper. Remove half of the marinade and set aside for a dipping sauce. Cut the chicken into strips and add them to the marinade. Cover and refrigerate for at least 1 hour, or overnight. (Reserve two tablespoons of the remaining half of the marinade for Round 2 Recipe: Spicy and Sweet Chicken Wraps, page 120.)

For the dipping sauce, whisk together the reserved marinade, peanut butter, and hot sauce. Cover and refrigerate until ready to serve.

Heat the grill. Cut the peppers into strips. Slice the zucchini and red onion. Brush the vegetables with some oil and season them with salt and pepper. Grill until the vegetables are charred and have softened a bit. Allow them to cool, then cut them into small pieces. While the vegetables are grilling, make the couscous according to package directions. When it is done, gently stir in the chopped vegetables. Cover, and keep warm. (Reserve 1 cup of couscous for Round 2 Recipe: Spicy and Sweet Chicken Wraps, page 120.)

Soak wooden skewers for at least 30 minutes to prevent burning. Remove the chicken from the marinade and discard the marinade. Thread the chicken onto skewers, and grill until charred and cooked through. (Reserve 4 skewers for Round 2 Recipe: Spicy and Sweet Chicken Wraps, page 120.) Serve with the dipping sauce and couscous.

Please see Round 2 Recipe on page 120

GRILLED FRUIT SKEWERS WITH SWEET YOGURT SAUCE

1	(20-ounce) can chunk pineapple (reserve the juice and 4 pieces for cocktail)	$1.25
2	nectarines, cut into 1-inch chunks	$0.60
1	mango, peeled, cored, and cut into 1-inch chunks	$0.99
1	pint strawberries	$1.25
½	cup brown sugar	$0.18
1	tsp. cinnamon	$0.09
1	orange (reserve juice of ½ orange for recipe, page 117; reserve half of zest for recipe, page 114)	$0.60
1	(8-ounce) container vanilla yogurt	$0.50

Soak wooden skewers in water for at least 30 minutes.

In a small pot, combine brown sugar with ¼ cup water, cinnamon, and zest of ½ orange. (Reserve zest of ½ orange for Chicken Satay with Grilled Vegetable Couscous, page 114. Reserve juice of ½ orange for Put a Stick in It Cocktail, page 117.) Bring to a boil, remove from heat, and set aside to cool to room temperature.

Preheat grill or grill pan over low heat.

Thread 2 pieces of each type of fruit onto each skewer. (Reserve 4 pieces and juice from canned pineapple chunks for Put a Stick in It Cocktail, page 117.) Grill the skewers until the fruit is warm and lightly charred, about 6 minutes, giving the skewers a quarter-turn every 1½ minutes. Make sure to brush with brown sugar syrup after each turn.

While the fruit is grilling, make the dipping sauce. Whisk together the yogurt, orange juice, and 1 tablespoon of the brown sugar liquid. (Reserve 2 tablespoons of sauce for Round 2 Recipe: Spicy and Sweet Chicken Wraps, page 120.) Transfer to serving bowl. Serve the skewers with the sauce on the side.

SERVES: 4
COOK TIME: 10 minutes
$5.46/$1.37 per person

Please see Round 2 Recipe on page 120

PUT A STICK IN IT COCKTAIL

1	liter ginger ale	$0.75
	Reserved pineapple juice	$0.00
	from canned pineapple chunks	
	(page 116)	
	Reserved juice of ½ orange	$0.00
	(page 116)	
4	maraschino cherries plus syrup	$0.20
	Reserved 4 pineapple chunks	$0.00
	(page 116)	
6	ounces rum, optional	$3.75

In a large pitcher, combine ginger ale, pineapple juice, orange juice, and 2 tablespoons of the maraschino syrup. Add rum if desired, and stir. Pour into glasses filled with ice.

Garnish with a cherry and a pineapple chunk on a skewer.

SERVES: 4
$0.95/$0.24 per person

SAUSAGE AND PEPPER BAKED ZITI

½	(16-ounce) package ziti	$0.50
2	tbsp. canola oil	$0.28
1	medium diced yellow onion	$0.28
2	tsp. chopped garlic	$0.04
1	tbsp. Italian seasoning	$0.18
1	(15-ounce) can crushed tomatoes	$0.89
	Reserved sausage and peppers (page 112)	$0.00
1	cup grated mozzarella	$1.00
	Kosher salt, to taste	$0.00
	Black pepper, to taste	$0.00

Heat the oven to 375°F. Bring a large pot of water to a boil. Coat a 9 × 13-inch baking pan lightly with oil. Cook the pasta for about 6 minutes. It should be under-cooked; it will finish cooking in the oven.

While pasta is cooking, heat oil in a large skillet over medium-high heat, add the onion and garlic, and sauté for about 3 minutes until slightly tender. Add tomatoes and Italian seasoning and cook for another 5 minutes. Chop up the sausage and peppers and add to the pan to heat through. Taste, and adjust the seasoning with salt and pepper.

Drain the pasta and add it to the prepared baking pan. Pour over the tomato sauce and top with the cheese. Bake until the cheese is melted and lightly browned, about 30 minutes.

TIP: *To make this dish ahead of time, place the uncooked baking dish in a freezer bag or wrap it lightly in plastic wrap and put it in the freezer. When you are ready to heat it up, add a few minutes to the cooking time.*

SERVES: 4
COOK TIME: 45 minutes
$3.17 in extra ingredients

Please see Main Recipe on page 112

SPICY AND SWEET CHICKEN WRAPS

1	head butter lettuce, leaves removed	$1.29
	Reserved 4 Chicken Satay Skewers, chopped (page 114)	$0.00
1	shredded carrot	$0.16
	Reserved Satay Dipping Sauce (page 114)	$0.00
	Reserved Sweet Yogurt Sauce (page 116)	$0.00
	Reserved couscous (page 114)	$0.00

Lay out the lettuce leaves on a clean, flat work surface. Evenly divide the chopped chicken, shredded carrot, and couscous between the leaves.

Whisk together the reserved Satay Dipping Sauce and Sweet Yogurt Sauce. Drizzle the sauce over the chicken, wrap it all up, and eat!

SERVES: 4

$1.45 in extra ingredients

Please see Main Recipes on pages 114 and 116

12. AFFORDABLE EASY ENTERTAINING

- A picture-perfect, sparkling cocktail party for a really great price!
- **Party total: $23.64/$3.94 per person**

    Crispy Baby Potato Bites with Sour Cream and Bacon,

    Chicken Sliders with Spicy BBQ Mayo, Cucumber Cups

    Stuffed with Shrimp Cocktail, and Sparkling Spritzer Bar

---

1. Crispy Baby Potato Bites with Sour Cream and Bacon

Total cost: $3.63/$0.60 per person

2. Chicken Sliders with Spicy BBQ Mayo

Total cost: $7.40/$1.23 per person

> **TIP:** *When slow-cooking chicken, it's best to use darker meat, because it won't dry out, and it's cheaper and more flavorful.*
>
> **TIP:** *Making your own sliders saves 50% over buying those hamburger sliders you find in the supermarket.*

> **MSM TIP:**
> Precooked bacon is 27% more expensive than bacon you cook yourself.

3. Cucumber Cups Stuffed with Shrimp Cocktail

Total cost: $7.51/$1.25 per person

4. Sparkling Spritzer Bar

Total cost: $5.10/$0.43 per person

> *Add an ounce of vodka for $0.53 per cocktail, or 4 ounces of prosecco for $1.56 per cocktail.*

> **MSM TIP:**
> Napa cabbage = $3.95 each
> Green cabbage = $1.74 each
> Savings = $1.95 or 52%

5. R2R: Chicken Tacos with Cucumber Salsa

$0.85 in extra ingredients

6. R2R: Potato and Shrimp Salad with Sour Cream and Bacon Dressing

$0.28 in extra ingredients

CRISPY BABY POTATO BITES WITH SOUR CREAM AND BACON

2	pounds new potatoes	$1.60
¼	cup canola oil	$0.12
1	tbsp. chopped rosemary	$0.02
8	strips bacon	$1.36
1	cup sour cream	$0.38
1	tbsp. spicy brown mustard	$0.04
2	tbsp. chopped chives	$0.11
	Kosher salt, to taste	$0.00
	Black pepper, to taste	$0.00

Heat the oven to 400°F.

Put the potatoes into a large pot and cover with cold water. Bring to a boil and add a generous pinch of salt. Let boil for 8 minutes so they are cooked but still slightly firm. Strain and let them cool. When they are cool enough to handle, cut them in half and carefully scoop out the insides using a teaspoon or melon baller to form a cup. (Reserve 6 whole potatoes and the scooped-out insides for Round 2 Recipe: Potato and Shrimp Salad with Sour Cream and Bacon Dressing, page 132.) Put potato cups in a bowl, add the oil, and season with salt and pepper. Carefully toss to coat them with the oil. Place the potatoes cut-side up on a baking sheet and sprinkle with rosemary. Bake until the cups are browned and crisp, about 15–20 minutes.

While the potatoes are baking, put the bacon into a skillet, and cook over medium heat until crisp. Drain the bacon well (reserve 2 strips for the Round 2 Recipe, page 132) and chop it.

In a bowl, stir together the sour cream, chopped bacon, mustard, 1 tablespoon chives, and salt and pepper to taste. Place the potatoes onto a serving plate and top each with a spoonful of the sour cream and bacon mixture. Garnish with the remaining chives and serve immediately.

SERVES: 6
COOK TIME: 30 minutes
$3.63/$0.60 per person

Please see Round 2 Recipe on page 132

CHICKEN SLIDERS WITH SPICY BBQ MAYO

1	medium chopped yellow onion	$0.28
1	tbsp. chopped garlic	$0.05
2	pounds bone-in, skin-on chicken thighs, about 8	$2.58
1	sprig fresh thyme	$0.01
1	sprig fresh rosemary	$0.01
½	cup mayonnaise	$0.24
½	cup barbecue sauce	$0.31
1	tbsp. spicy brown mustard	$0.04
1	tbsp. hot sauce	$0.06
1	head shredded green cabbage	$1.74
1	tbsp. apple cider vinegar	$0.03
2	tsp. sugar	$0.01
½	tsp. red pepper flakes	$0.04
1	dozen small dinner rolls	$2.00
	Kosher salt, to taste	$0.00
	Black pepper, to taste	$0.00

In a heavy-bottomed pot with a tight-fitting lid, add the onion and garlic. Add the chicken thighs, skin-side down, fitting them in tightly. Add the thyme and rosemary sprigs, season with salt and pepper, and pour over ½ cup water. Put the pot over medium-high heat. When it comes to a boil, lower the heat, cover, and simmer for 1 hour. Remove the chicken from the pot and let it cool. When it is cool, shred the meat (reserve 2 thighs for Round 2 Recipe: Chicken Tacos with Cucumber Salsa, page 130), discarding the skin and bones.

While the chicken is cooking, whisk together in a bowl the mayonnaise, barbecue sauce, mustard, and hot sauce. Taste, and adjust the seasoning with salt and pepper. Cover and refrigerate until ready to use.

In another bowl, toss together the cabbage (reserve 1 cup of cabbage for Round 2 Recipe: Chicken Tacos with Cucumber Salsa, page 130), vinegar, sugar, and red pepper flakes. Season with salt and pepper, cover, and refrigerate until ready to use.

To serve, split the rolls and spread a heaping teaspoon of the flavored mayo onto each roll top and bottom. Divide the shredded chicken and put it onto each roll bottom. Put some cabbage on top, cover, and insert a toothpick to hold it all together.

Please see Round 2 Recipe on page 130

SERVES: 6
COOK TIME: 1 hour
$7.40/$1.23 per person

CUCUMBER CUPS STUFFED WITH SHRIMP COCKTAIL

2	cucumbers	$1.50
¾	pound medium shrimp, cooked	$4.87
1	(15-ounce) can chopped tomatoes, drained	$0.99
1	tbsp. horseradish	$0.10
1	tsp. lemon juice	$0.03
1	tbsp. chopped fresh parsley, plus leaves for garnish	$0.02
	Kosher salt, to taste	$0.00
	Black pepper, to taste	$0.00

Peel the length of the cucumber to form alternating stripes of light and dark. Cut the cucumber into 12 (¾-inch) pieces. Scoop out the seeds using a teaspoon or melon baller, leaving the bottom and sides intact to form a cup. Discard the seeds. (Reserve the remaining cucumber for the Round 2 Recipe: Chicken Tacos with Cucumber Salsa, page 130.) Turn them upside down and let them drain on a towel while you make the filling.

Chop the shrimp into small pieces and put them into a bowl. (Reserve ½ cup chopped shrimp for the Round 2 Recipe: Potato and Shrimp Salad with Sour Cream and Bacon Dressing, page 132.) Add half the tomatoes (reserve the remaining tomatoes for the Round 2 Recipe: Chicken Tacos with Cucumber Salsa, page 130), the horseradish, lemon juice, parsley, and salt and pepper to taste. Spoon the shrimp mixture into the cucumber cups and top each with a parsley leaf.

SERVES: 6
$7.51/$1.25 per person

Please see Round 2 Recipes on pages 130 and 132

SPARKLING SPRITZER BAR

3	cups sugar	$0.60
1	orange, zested in strips and sliced	$0.50
8	sprigs fresh mint	$0.10
1	lime, zested in strips and sliced	$0.33
1	piece (1-inch) ginger, peeled and sliced	$0.25
1	cup frozen raspberries	$2.00
4	bottles sparkling water	$1.32
2	bottles prosecco, optional	$19.90
1	bottle flavored vodka, optional	$13.50

In bowl add orange zest and 4 sprigs of mint. In a second bowl add lime zest and ginger. To a third bowl add ¾ cup of the raspberries.

In a pot mix the sugar and 3 cups water. Place over medium heat and bring it to a boil then evenly divide the sugar syrup among the 3 bowls. Stir each to mix and let cool to room temperature. Pour each into jars or syrup containers and refrigerate until ready to use or up to 2 weeks.

To Set Up the Spritzer Bar:
Set out chilled bottles of sparkling water. Put out plenty of champagne flutes or wineglasses. Let people create their own Sparkling Spritzer by mixing about 3 tablespoons of a flavored syrup with some sparkling water and a shot of vodka or prosecco if desired. Garnish drinks with mint sprigs, oranges slices, or lime slices.

SERVES: 12
COOK TIME: 5 minutes
$5.10/$0.43 per person

CHICKEN TACOS WITH CUCUMBER SALSA

2	tbsp. canola oil	$0.06
1	chopped red onion (reserve half for Round 2 Recipe, page 132)	$0.67
½	tsp. red pepper flakes	$0.04
½	tsp. chili powder	$0.01
	Reserved shredded chicken thighs (page 126)	$0.00
	Reserved chopped cucumber (page 128)	$0.00
	Reserved tomatoes (page 128)	$0.00
1	tbsp. chopped fresh cilantro	$0.02
8	crispy taco shells	$0.00
	Reserved shredded cabbage (page 126)	$0.00
2	tbsp. sour cream	$0.05
	Kosher salt, to taste	$0.00
	Black pepper, to taste	$0.00

In a skillet over medium heat, add the oil. Sauté half the onion, red pepper flakes, and chili powder until the onions are soft, about 5 minutes. Add the chicken and cook until it is warmed through, about 5 minutes. (Reserve half of chopped red onion for Round 2 Recipe: Potato and Shrimp Salad with Sour Cream and Bacon Dressing, page 132.)

For the salsa, in a bowl mix together the cucumber, tomatoes, remaining onion, cilantro, and salt and pepper to taste.

Spoon the chicken mixture into the taco shells, top with the salsa, cabbage, and sour cream.

SERVES: 4
COOK TIME: 10 minutes
$0.85 in extra ingredients

Please see Main Recipe on page 126

POTATO AND SHRIMP SALAD WITH SOUR CREAM AND BACON DRESSING

3	tbsp. sour cream	$0.07
1	tbsp. spicy brown mustard	$0.04
	Reserved ½ chopped red onion (page 130)	$0.00
1	tbsp. chopped fresh parsley	$0.02
	Reserved potatoes, chopped (page 124)	$0.00
	Reserved chopped shrimp (page 124)	$0.00
1	stalk chopped celery	$0.15
	Reserved 2 strips bacon, chopped (page 124)	$0.00
	Kosher salt, to taste	$0.00
	Black pepper, to taste	$0.00

In a bowl, whisk together the sour cream, mustard, onion, parsley, and salt and pepper to taste. Add the potato, shrimp, celery, and bacon. Toss everything together until it is all coated with the dressing.

SERVES: 4

$0.28 in extra ingredients

Please see Main Recipe on page 124

13. BRUNCH FOR A BUNCH

- **Meal total: $17.62/$4.41 per person**
  Asparagus and Tomato Tart, French Toast with Brown-Sugar Banana Syrup, Mini Apple Spice Glazed Donuts, and Sparkling Cider Mimosa

1. Asparagus and Tomato Tart
Total cost: $5.87/$0.73 per person

2. French Toast with Brown-Sugar Banana Syrup
Total cost: $6.04/$1.51 per person

3. Mini Apple Spice Glazed Donuts
Total cost: $2.60/$0.65 per person

4. Sparkling Cider Mimosa
Total cost: $3.13/$0.78 per person

5. R2R: Cream of Asparagus Soup
$2.53 in extra ingredients

6. R2R: Bread Pudding
$0.76 in extra ingredients

MSM TIP:
Fresh asparagus in season will cost you $1.69 a bunch/$3.69 cheaper than frozen.

MSM TIP:
Sandra's Brown Sugar and Banana Syrup = $1.52
Store-bought maple syrup = $5.11
Savings = $3.59

ASPARAGUS AND TOMATO TART

1	9-inch frozen piecrust	$1.65
½	cup ricotta cheese	$0.44
¼	cup milk	S0.06
2	eggs, lightly beaten	$0.34
1	tbsp. chopped fresh basil	$0.01
1	tbsp. chopped fresh parsley	$0.01
2	slices of bacon, chopped	$0.34
1	small yellow onion, chopped	$0.28
½	bunch fresh asparagus, ends removed, chopped (reserve stems and stalks for Round 2 Recipe, page 144)	$1.69
1	(14.5-ounce) can diced tomatoes with Italian herbs, drained well	$0.99
1	tsp. balsamic vinegar	$0.06
½	tsp. kosher salt	$0.00
¼	tsp. black pepper	$0.00

Preheat oven to 375°F.
Par-bake the piecrust for 10 minutes.

Sauté the bacon in a skillet until crisp. Remove bacon and drain on paper towel. Add onion and asparagus to the skillet with the bacon fat. Sauté until onions are soft, approximately 5 minutes.

Stir together ricotta, milk, eggs, parsley, ½ tablespoon basil, and salt and pepper in a medium mixing bowl until combined. Arrange asparagus, onions, and half the tomatoes in the piecrust. Pour egg mixture into prepared crust.

Bake in oven for 40–45 minutes or until eggs have set and the tart is puffed up and lightly browned on top. Remove from oven and let cool for 5 minutes. Serve warm or at room temperature.

In a small bowl, toss the remaining tomatoes with the remaining basil and balsamic vinegar, and season with salt and pepper. Serve over tart.

SERVES: 8
COOKING TIME: 10 minutes
$5.87/$0.73 per person

Please see Round 2 Recipe on page 144

FRENCH TOAST WITH BROWN-SUGAR BANANA SYRUP

SYRUP: $1.52

2	tbsp. butter	$0.12
½	tsp. pumpkin pie spice	$0.25
2	tbsp. molasses	$0.37
½	cup brown sugar	$0.20
2	bananas, sliced into	$0.58
	½ inch slices	

FRENCH TOAST: $4.52

	Fresh challah	$2.90
2	cups milk	$0.48
3	large eggs	$0.51
½	cup flour	$0.08
2	tsp. vanilla extract	$0.41
2	tbsp. light brown sugar	$0.05
¼	tsp. salt	$0.00

SERVES: 4

COOK TIME: 15 minutes

$6.04/$1.51 per person

FOR SYRUP:

In a small saucepan, combine butter, pumpkin pie spice, molasses, brown sugar, and ½ cup of water. Bring to a boil, add bananas then lower heat and let simmer 3 minutes. Remove syrup from heat, cover and keep warm. Serve over French toast, and save extra for Round 2 Recipe, p. 146. Also makes a great topping for ice cream.

FOR FRENCH TOAST:

Preheat oven to 400°F.

Slice bread into 12 slices. Reserve two slices plus the ends for the bread pudding Round 2 Recipe. Place remaining eight slices onto a baking sheet. Toast in oven for 3 minutes. Remove and lower oven to 250°F.

In a large bowl whisk together the milk, eggs, flour, vanilla, brown sugar, and salt.

Spray a 12-inch skillet with nonstick cooking spray and place over medium heat. Working in batches of four, dip the bread into the batter and soak both sides. Remove, allowing excess to drip back into the bowl and lay in the hot skillet. Cook until golden brown on both sides, about 3 minutes per side. Transfer the French toast to a baking sheet fitted with a wire rack and keep warm in a 250-degree oven. Repeat with remaining slices of bread. Save remaining batter for bread pudding Round 2 Recipe.

Please see Round 2 Recipe on page 146

MINI APPLE SPICE GLAZED DONUTS

1	can (7.5-ounce) refrigerator biscuits	$0.59/can
3	cups canola oil	$1.44
1	cup powdered sugar	$0.28
½	tsp. pumpkin pie spice	$0.25
2	tbsp. apple juice	$0.04

Remove the biscuits from the can and place onto a cutting board. Using a half-inch biscuit cutter or the cap from a water bottle, remove the center from each biscuit. Place both the donuts and donut holes onto a sheet pan and allow them to rest and come to temperature, about 15 minutes.

In a large bowl, combine powdered sugar, pumpkin pie spice, and apple juice. Whisk together until smooth and well combined. Set aside while the donuts fry.

Heat the oil in a medium pot to 350°F. Fry the donuts three at a time until golden brown, about 1 minute per side. Remove from oil and place on a sheet tray lined with a paper towel. Repeat with remaining donuts and donut holes.

Dip the top of each donut into the prepared glaze and place onto a serving tray. Let glaze set about 5 minutes.

MAKES: 10 donuts and 10 donut holes
COOK TIME: 5 minutes
$2.60/ $0.65 per person

SPARKLING CIDER MIMOSA

1	bottle sparkling apple cider	$2.49
1	cup cranberry juice	$0.40
½	cup orange juice	$0.24

Combine all ingredients in a pitcher and pour into chilled champagne flutes.

SERVES: 4
$3.13/$0.78 per person

CREAM OF ASPARAGUS SOUP

2	tbsp. canola oil	$0.06
	Reserved asparagus stems and stalks (page 136)	$0.00
½	small yellow onion	$0.18
2	cups milk	$0.50
1	tbsp. chopped fresh parsley	$0.01
1	can (10.75-ounce) cream of potato soup	$1.69
2	tbsp. sour cream	$0.09
	Kosher salt, to taste	$0.00
	Black pepper, to taste	$0.00

Add oil to a medium pot over medium heat. Add onions and asparagus and sauté for five minutes. Add milk and parsley and bring to a simmer. Reduce heat to low and let simmer for five minutes.

Carefully pour into blender, add the cream of potato soup, and puree. Pour back into pot through a fine-mesh strainer.

Return the pot to medium heat. Whisk in the sour cream and season with salt and pepper. Bring to a simmer. Remove from heat and serve.

SERVES: 4

COOK TIME: 12 minutes

$2.53 in extra ingredients

Please see Main Recipe on page 136

BREAD PUDDING

4	slices of leftover challah bread French toast, cut into cubes	$0.00
1	egg	$0.17
1	cup milk	$0.24
	Reserved French toast batter	$0.00
½	tsp. pumpkin pie spice	$0.25
¼	cup light brown sugar	$0.10
	Reserved brown-sugar banana syrup	

Preheat oven to 325°F.

Spray four 7-ounce ramekins with nonstick cooking spray. Place onto a baking sheet and set aside.

In a large bowl combine egg, milk, pumpkin pie spice, brown sugar, and extra French toast batter. Whisk together until well blended. Add bread and mix so that all the bread is coated. Cover and let sit for 30 minutes–1 hour in the refrigerator.

Evenly divide the bread and batter mixture among the four ramekins. Place in oven and bake for 30–40 minutes or until set.

Serve warm and top with extra brown-sugar banana syrup.

SERVES: 4

COOK TIME: 40 minutes

$0.76 in extra ingredients

Please see Main Recipe on page 138

Pair with a
Banana Daiquiri
(page 225)

14. A BOUNTIFUL HARVEST

- A Thanksgiving feast that will warm the hearts of your family and friends and save you money.
- I love to entertain, and Thanksgiving is the most important gathering for me. It is a time to be with the people most dear to you. Show them how much you care by preparing a delicious meal.
- **Meal total: $46.20/$5.77 per person**

   Roasted Turkey Breast with Spicy Herb Oil, Golden Raisin and Walnut Stuffing, Baked Mashed Potatoes, Pumpkin Mousse, and a Pumpkin Pie Martini

1. Roasted Turkey Breast with Spicy Herb Oil

Total cost: $22.77/$2.85 per person

Purchasing an entire turkey and using every part is more economical than buying it in portions. Larger, meatier birds—about 15 pounds—are less expensive per pound than smaller hens. (Smaller turkeys stay more moist.)

MSM TIP:
Walnuts are 36% cheaper than pecans.

2. Golden Raisin and Walnut Stuffing

Total cost: $6.44/$0.81 per person

3. Baked Mashed Potatoes

Total cost: $7.88/$0.98 per person

4. Pumpkin Mousse

Total cost: $6.47/$0.81 per person

MSM TIP:
Per pound, dried cranberries are $1.32 vs. $0.48 for raisins— savings: $0.84 or 64% if you use raisins.

5. Pumpkin Pie Martini

Total cost: $2.64/$0.33 per mocktail

6. R2R: Turkey Soup

$1.36 in extra ingredients

7. R2R: Fried Potato Cakes

$0.62 in extra ingredients

ROASTED TURKEY BREAST WITH SPICY HERB OIL

¼	cup canola oil	$0.12
1	tbsp. chopped fresh sage	$0.02
1	tbsp. chopped fresh thyme	$0.02
2	tsp. chopped fresh rosemary	$0.01
2	tsp. garlic powder	$0.10
1	tsp. paprika	$0.08
½	tsp. chili powder	$0.01
½	tsp. red pepper flakes	$0.04
1	(13-pound) fresh turkey	$21.97
1	cup chicken broth	$0.40
	Kosher salt, to taste	$0.00
	Black pepper, to taste	$0.00

In a bowl stir together the oil, sage, thyme, rosemary, garlic powder, paprika, chili powder, and red pepper flakes. Set aside.

Remove the legs, thighs, and wings from the turkey (reserve for Round 2 Recipe, page 160). Season the breast well with salt and pepper. Rub the herb oil all over turkey, making sure to get under the skin as well. Place on a rack in a roasting pan, cover, and let it sit at room temperature to marinate for 30 minutes.

Preheat the oven to 350°F.

Uncover, pour the broth into the bottom of the pan, and roast the turkey breast until it is almost cooked. A thermometer inserted in the thickest part should read 110 to 120°F, about 55–60 minutes. Increase the oven temperature to 450°F and cook until the skin is browned and a thermometer inserted in the thickest part reads 160 to 165°F, about 15–20 minutes. Let rest for 10 minutes before carving.

SERVES: 8
COOK TIME: 1 hour 20 minutes
$22.77/$2.85 per person

Please see Round 2 Recipe on page 160

GOLDEN RAISIN AND WALNUT STUFFING

	Nonstick cooking spray	$0.00
¾	cup golden raisins	$0.48
2	tbsp. canola oil	$0.06
1	medium chopped yellow onion	$0.28
3	chopped celery stalks	$0.45
1	loaf stale bread, cubed and toasted	$1.69
2	tsp. poultry seasoning	$0.06
¼	cup chopped fresh parsley	$0.08
2	tbsp. chopped fresh sage	$0.04
1	cup walnuts, toasted and coarsely chopped	$1.72
2	(14.5-ounce) cans chicken broth	$1.58
	Kosher salt, to taste	$0.00
	Black pepper, to taste	$0.00

Preheat the oven to 350°F. Spray a 9 × 13-inch baking dish with cooking spray. Place the raisins in a small bowl and cover with 1 cup hot water. Set aside.

In a large skillet over medium heat, add the oil. When it is hot, add the onion and celery, season with salt and pepper, and cook until softened, about 6–7 minutes.

Drain the raisins, reserving the liquid, and put them into a large bowl with the bread, onions, celery, poultry seasoning, parsley, sage, and walnuts. Mix everything together, pour over 1½ cans broth, season with salt and pepper, and mix again. If the mixture seems too dry, add some of the reserved soaking liquid from the raisins. Spoon the stuffing into the prepared baking dish (stuffing can be made ahead to this point, covered, and refrigerated overnight). Bake until the top is golden brown, about 25–30 minutes.

SERVES: 8
COOK TIME: 40 minutes
$6.44/$0.81 per person

BAKED MASHED POTATOES

6	strips bacon	$1.02
	Fresh bread crumbs from	$0.80
	10 slices white bread	
	Nonstick cooking spray	$0.00
2	cups milk	$0.32
4	tbsp. unsalted butter	$0.24
5	pounds russet potatoes	$3.49
4	ounces cream cheese, at	$0.68
	room temperature	
1	cup shredded Cheddar cheese	$1.00
3	tbsp. fresh chopped chives	$0.33
	Kosher salt, to taste	$0.00
	Black pepper, to taste	$0.00

SERVES: 8
COOK TIME: 1 hour
$7.88/$0.98 per person

In a large skillet over medium heat, cook the bacon until crisp. Drain on brown paper. Remove all but 1 tablespoon of fat from the pan. (Reserve 1 cup bread crumbs for Round 2 Recipe, page 162.) Add the remaining bread crumbs and cook until they are lightly toasted, about 5 minutes. Set aside.

Preheat the oven to 350°F. Spray a 9 x 3-inch baking dish with nonstick spray. In a small saucepan over low heat, warm the milk and butter.

Wash the potatoes well, cut them into 1-inch cubes, and put them into a large pot. Cover the potatoes with water, add salt, put the pot over high heat, and bring it to a boil. When the potatoes are cooked through, about 20 minutes, strain them, put them back into the pot, and mash them. (Reserve 2 cups mashed potatoes for Round 2 Recipe, page 162.)

Add the cream cheese to the potatoes and continue to mash. Slowly stir in the warm milk just until incorporated and fold in the grated cheese. Overmixing the potatoes will cause them to become gluey. Season to taste with salt and pepper.

Put the potatoes into the prepared baking dish, crumble the bacon over the top, and sprinkle evenly with the bread crumbs. Bake until heated through and golden brown on top, about 25–30 minutes. Serve garnished with chives.

Please see Round 2 Recipe on page 162

PUMPKIN MOUSSE

1	(15-ounce) can pumpkin puree	**$1.59**
½	cup brown sugar	**$0.18**
1½	tsp. pumpkin pie spice	**$0.45**
1	tsp. vanilla	**$0.44**
2½	cups heavy cream, chilled	**$2.80**
1	tbsp. granulated sugar	**$0.01**
4	ounces cream cheese	**$1.00**

In a large bowl, using an electric hand mixer, beat the cream cheese, pumpkin puree, brown sugar, 1 teaspoon pumpkin pie spice, and vanilla until it becomes smooth and creamy. (Reserve 2 tbsp. of the pumpkin puree for the Pumpkin Pie Martini, page 158.)

In another large bowl, using an electric hand mixer, beat 2 cups of the cream until it forms soft peaks. Add ¼ of the whipped cream to the pumpkin mixture and stir to lighten it. Gently fold in the remaining whipped cream. Spoon the mousse into dessert glasses, cover, and refrigerate for at least 2 hours or overnight.

When you are ready to serve, whip the remaining cream with the granulated sugar. Top each mousse with a dollop of whipped cream and a sprinkling of the remaining ½ teaspoon pumpkin pie spice.

SERVES: 8
$6.47/$0.81 per person

PUMPKIN PIE MARTINI

½	cup brown sugar	$0.18
2	tsp. pumpkin pie spice	$0.60
2	tbsp. granulated sugar	$0.03
2	cups half and half	$1.28
	Reserved pumpkin puree (page 156)	$0.00
½	tsp. vanilla extract	$0.22
1	liter sparkling water	$0.33
4	ounces vanilla vodka, optional	$2.12

In a small saucepan over medium heat, combine the brown sugar, 1 teaspoon pumpkin pie spice, and ½ cup of water. Stir until the sugar is dissolved and bring to a boil. Remove from heat and cool. Pour into a clean jar, cover, and store in the refrigerator until you are ready to use it, for up to 2 weeks.

Mix together the granulated sugar and remaining 1 teaspoon pumpkin pie spice, and put it onto a shallow plate. Put a little water onto another plate. Dip the rims of martini glasses in the water, then in the spiced sugar. Set aside.

Whisk together the half and half, pumpkin puree, and vanilla, and blend until combined. Fill a cocktail shaker with ice, and add 2 tablespoons of the spiced syrup and ½ cup of the cream mixture. Shake well and pour into the prepared glasses. Top with sparkling water. If using the vodka, add it to the shaker before shaking.

SERVES: 8
COOK TIME: 5 minutes
$2.64/$0.33 per person

TURKEY SOUP

	Reserved turkey parts	$0.00
3	sprigs of fresh thyme	$0.03
2	bay leaves	$0.07
2	tbsp. canola oil	$0.06
1	chopped medium onion	$0.28
2	chopped stalks celery	$0.30
1	chopped carrot	$0.16
1	parsnip, cut in half and sliced	$0.33
1	tbsp. chopped garlic	$0.05
¼	cup chopped fresh parsley	$0.08
	Kosher salt, to taste	$0.00
	Black pepper, to taste	$0.00

In a large pot over high heat, add the turkey parts and cover with 4 quarts of water. Add the thyme, bay leaves, and a big pinch of salt, and bring to a boil. Reduce the heat to simmer, skimming any scum that rises to the surface. Cook until the turkey is cooked through and the liquid has reduced a bit, about 45 minutes. Remove the turkey from the pot. When it is cool enough to handle, shred the meat and discard the skin and bones. Strain the broth.

Wipe out the pot, put it over medium-high heat, and add the oil. When it is hot, add the onions, celery, carrot, and parsnip, season with salt and pepper, and cook until softened, about 7–8 minutes. Add the garlic and cook for another minute. Add the turkey broth and bring to a simmer. Add the meat to the pot and let it simmer to warm through, about 10 minutes. Remove from the heat. Stir in the parsley just before serving.

SERVES: 8

COOK TIME: 1 hour

$1.36 in extra ingredients

Please see Main Recipe on page 150

FRIED POTATO CAKES

	Reserved bread crumbs (page 154)	$0.00
	Reserved mashed potatoes (page 154)	$0.00
¼	cup shredded mozzarella cheese	$0.25
1	large egg, beaten	$0.11
⅛	tsp. cayenne pepper	$0.02
½	cup canola oil	$0.24
	Kosher salt, to taste	$0.00
	Black pepper, to taste	$0.00

In a shallow plate or pie dish, mix the bread crumbs with salt and pepper, to taste. In a large bowl, stir together the potatoes, cheese, egg, cayenne pepper, and salt and pepper, to taste. Scoop out ¼ cup of the potato mixture and form it into a small patty. Gently press the patties into the seasoned bread crumbs, coating both sides, and set aside.

In a large skillet over medium heat, add the oil. When it is hot, add the potato cakes in 1 layer and cook until golden brown and crispy, about 2 minutes per side. Drain on brown paper and sprinkle with more salt and pepper while hot.

SERVES: 4
COOK TIME: 5 minutes
$0.62 in extra ingredients

Please see Main Recipe on page 154

15. THE HOLIDAY HELPER

- Cooking a delicious meal, and sharing it with your family and friends, is one of my favorite things about the season . . . and it can be done inexpensively.
- **You could have this entire holiday feast, which serves six people, for just $20.20. That is just $3.37 per person for a meal that will really bring joy to the holiday season.**
- Meal total: $20.20/$3.37 per person

  Roast Bone-in Pork Loin with Apple Mustard Glaze, Mixed Roasted Potatoes with Herb Butter, Cheesy Creamed Spinach, Eggnog Custard Cups, and Cranberry Orange Ho-Ho-jitos

---

1. Roast Bone-in Pork Loin with Apple Mustard Glaze

Total cost: $8.13/$1.36 per person

2. Mixed Roasted Potatoes with Herb Butter

Total cost: $4.60/$0.77 per person

3. Cheesy Creamed Spinach

Total cost: $3.13/$0.52 per person

> **MSM TIP:**
> Beef rib roast = $8.99/lb
> Pork rib loin = $1.49/lb
> Savings = $7.50 or 82%

4. Eggnog Custard Cups

Total cost: $1.90/$0.32 per person

5. Cranberry Orange Ho-Ho-jitos

Total cost: $2.44/$0.41 per person

Add an ounce of white rum for another $0.42 to turn your mocktail into a cocktail

> **MSM TIP:**
> Cream = $2.24
> Whole milk = $0.32
> Savings = $1.92 or 86%

6. R2R: Pork Hash

$0.88 in extra ingredients

7. R2R: Spinach and Cheese Soufflé

$0.44 in extra ingredients

ROAST BONE-IN PORK LOIN WITH APPLE MUSTARD GLAZE

1	(4½-to-5½-pound) bone-in pork loin roast	$7.45
1½	cups apple juice	$0.36
3	tbsp. spicy brown mustard	$0.13
2	tbsp. brown sugar	$0.04
1	tbsp. Worcestershire sauce	$0.06
1	tbsp. soy sauce	$0.09
	Kosher salt, to taste	$0.00
	Black pepper, to taste	$0.00

Heat the oven to 350°F. Allow the pork to come to room temperature.

Place the roast fat-side up on a rack in a roasting pan, and season with salt and pepper. Put in the oven and roast for 1 hour. Meanwhile, make the glaze.

In a saucepan over medium-high heat, bring the apple juice to a boil and reduce it by half, about 10 minutes. Whisk in the mustard, brown sugar, Worcestershire sauce, and soy sauce, and reduce by half, about 5 more minutes. When the pork loin has been roasting for 1 hour, start brushing it with the glaze every 15 minutes. Cook until the roast reaches an internal temperature of 150°F, about 2 hours total. Remove the roast from the oven, give it another coating of glaze, and let it rest, uncovered, for 15 minutes before carving. (Reserve 1 cup of the meat for the Round 2 Recipe: Pork Hash, page 174.)

SERVES: 6
COOK TIME: 2 hours, 10 minutes
$8.13/$1.36 per person

Please see Round 2 Recipe on page 174

MIXED ROASTED POTATOES WITH HERB BUTTER

1½	pounds russet potatoes	$1.10
1½	pounds red potatoes	$1.20
2	pounds sweet potatoes	$1.98
1	tbsp. canola oil	$0.03
¼	cup unsalted butter, at room temperature	$0.24
1	tbsp. chopped fresh parsley	$0.02
1	tbsp. chopped fresh thyme	$0.02
½	tbsp. chopped fresh rosemary	$0.01
	Kosher salt, to taste	$0.00
	Black pepper, to taste	$0.00

Cut all the potatoes into 2-inch cubes. Add them to a large pot, cover with water, and add salt. Bring them to a boil, cook for 10 minutes, drain, and cool. The potatoes will be only partially cooked and should be completely dry before you roast them.

Heat the oven to 400°F.

Toss the potatoes with the oil and spread them in one layer on a baking sheet. Roast until crispy and cooked through, about 45 minutes.

While the potatoes are roasting, make the herb butter: Mix the softened butter with the parsley, thyme, and rosemary, and season it with salt and pepper to taste.

When the potatoes are done, put them into a large bowl (reserve 1 cup for the Round 2 Recipe: Pork Hash, page 174) and toss with herb butter. (Reserve 2 tablespoons butter for the Round 2 Recipe: Pork Hash, page 174.) Serve immediately.

SERVES: 6
COOK TIME: 1 hour 15 minutes
$4.60/$0.77 per person

Please see Round 2 Recipe on page 174

CHEESY CREAMED SPINACH

2	(10-ounce) packages frozen chopped spinach, thawed	$1.98
2	tbsp. unsalted butter	$0.12
2	tbsp. all-purpose flour	$0.02
2	cups milk	$0.32
½	tsp. pumpkin pie spice	$0.15
¼	cup grated Parmesan cheese	$0.54
	Kosher salt, to taste	$0.00
	Black pepper, to taste	$0.00

Squeeze the spinach to get rid of all the excess water. Set aside.

In a small saucepan over medium heat, warm the milk. In a medium saucepan over medium heat, melt the butter. Whisk the flour into the butter and cook for 2 minutes. Whisk in the warm milk a bit at a time to avoid lumps. Cook until the sauce begins to thicken, about 2–3 minutes. Add the pumpkin pie spice and a pinch of salt. Turn the heat to low, stir in the cheese, and let melt. Stir in the spinach and cook for another 2–3 minutes to heat it through. (Save 1 cup of creamed spinach for Round 2 Recipe: Spinach and Cheese Soufflé, page 176.)

SERVES: 6
COOK TIME: 10 minutes
$3.13/$0.52 per person

Please see Round 2 Recipe on page 176

EGGNOG CUSTARD CUPS

2½	cups milk	$0.40
3	large eggs	$0.33
3	large egg yolks (reserve 3 egg whites for the Round 2 Recipe, page 176)	$0.33
½	cup sugar	$0.10
1	tsp. pumpkin pie spice	$0.30
1	tsp. vanilla extract	$0.44
½	tsp. salt	$0.00

Heat the oven to 325°F.

In a small pot over medium heat, add the milk. Whisk together the 3 eggs and 3 yolks. Whisk in the sugar, half the pumpkin pie spice, salt, and vanilla. Slowly whisk the warm milk into the egg mixture. Pour the liquid into six 8-ounce ovenproof ramekins, and sprinkle the remaining pumpkin pie spice on top. Place the cups in a baking dish and put the dish in the oven. Pour hot tap water into the baking dish to come about halfway up the sides of the cups. Bake for 35–40 minutes or until the custard is set around the edges and just jiggles slightly in the middle. Remove from the oven and let cool in the water bath. Refrigerate.

SERVES: 6
COOK TIME: 45 minutes
$1.90/$0.32 per person

CRANBERRY ORANGE HO-HO-JITOS

½	(12-ounce) bag cranberries, plus more for garnish	$1.40
1	orange, sliced, saving some for garnish	$0.50
1	bunch mint, saving some sprigs for garnish	$0.10
½	cup sugar	$0.10
1	liter sparkling water	$0.34
4	ounces white rum, optional	$1.70

In a large pitcher, add the cranberries, orange, mint, and sugar. Muddle them with the back of a wooden spoon, working out the juices of the fruit and dissolving the sugar. Add the sparkling water and stir to combine. Pour the mixture over ice and garnish with a slice of orange, some cranberries, and a sprig of mint. For the adults, add the white rum.

SERVES: 6
$2.44/$0.41 per person

Please see Round 2 Recipe on page 176

PORK HASH

1	tbsp. canola oil	$0.03
1	medium chopped yellow onion	$0.28
1	chopped green bell pepper	$0.48
½	tsp. red pepper flakes	$0.04
1	tbsp. chopped garlic	$0.05
	Reserved chopped potatoes (page 168)	$0.00
	Reserved chopped pork (page 166)	$0.00
	Reserved herb butter (page 168)	$0.00
	Kosher salt, to taste	$0.00
	Black pepper, to taste	$0.00

Heat a cast-iron skillet over medium-high heat with the oil. Add the onion, pepper, red pepper flakes, salt and pepper to taste, and cook until the vegetables are softened, about 6–8 minutes. Add the garlic and cook for 30 seconds. Add the potatoes and pork and cook for 5 minutes to heat them through. Add the reserved herb butter and cook until the hash is hot and crispy, about another 5 minutes.

SERVES: 4

COOK TIME: 10 minutes

$0.88 in extra ingredients

Please see Main Recipes on pages 166 and 168

SPINACH AND CHEESE SOUFFLÉ

	Nonstick cooking spray	$0.00
	Reserved Creamed Spinach (page 170)	$0.00
¼	cup shredded Monterey Jack cheese	$0.44
	Reserved 3 egg whites, (page 172)	$0.00

Heat oven to 375°F. Spray four 8-ounce ramekins with the cooking spray.

In a bowl, mix the creamed spinach to lighten it a bit, then add the cheese. Put the egg whites into another bowl and, using an electric hand mixer, whisk them until they are able to hold stiff peaks but are still glossy. Add a third of the egg whites to the spinach and mix in to lighten it. Fold in the remaining egg whites. Divide the mixture among the ramekins. Place them on a baking sheet and bake until they are risen, set, and golden brown, about 25–30 minutes. Serve immediately.

SERVES: 4

COOK TIME: 30 minutes

$0.44 in extra ingredients

Please see Main Recipes on pages 170 and 172

16. LESS IS MORE

- A special dinner that brings your family around the table.
- **Meal total: $30.38/$7.60 per person**
    Pan-Fried Tilapia, Beef Kebabs, and
    Coconut Caramel Cream Pie

1. Pan-Fried Tilapia with Sautéed Edamame
Total cost: $12.90/$3.23 per person

Total cost for Tilapia: $11.11/$2.78 per person

Total cost for Edamame: $1.79/$0.45 per person

TIP: *All-purpose seafood seasoning is one of my pantry staples—it is tasty and cost-effective.*

2. Beef Kebabs with Spicy Couscous
Total cost: $12.19/$3.05 per person

Total cost for Beef Kebabs: $9.34/$2.34 per person

Total cost for Spicy Couscous: $2.85/$0.71 per person

3. Coconut Caramel Cream Pie
Total cost: $5.29/$0.66 per person

4. R2R: Beef Kebab Pita Pockets
$1.14 in extra ingredients

5. R2R: Bow Ties and Buttons
$1.28 in extra ingredients

MSM TIP:
Tilapia = $6.99/lb
Cod = $10.99/lb
Halibut = $14.99/lb

MSM TIP:
Bottom Round = $2.49/lb
Sirloin Steak = $6.49/lb

MSM TIP:
Store-bought caramel sauce = $1.20
Caramel sauce from scratch = $0.56
Savings = $0.64

MSM TIP:
Coconut milk = $0.40
Heavy cream = $0.75
Savings = $0.35

MSM TIP:
Store-bought piecrust = $1.49
Piecrust from scratch = $2.19
Savings = $0.70

PAN-FRIED TILAPIA WITH SAUTÉED EDAMAME

TILAPIA

1½	pounds fresh tilapia fillets	$10.50
¼	cup all-purpose flour	$0.04
2	tsp. seafood seasoning	$0.20
2	tbsp. canola oil	$0.09
1	tbsp. chopped garlic	$0.05
2	tbsp. butter	$0.12
2	tbsp. lemon juice	$0.07
2	tbsp. chopped fresh parsley	$0.04
1	tsp. salt	$0.00
½	tsp. black pepper	$0.00

Heat oven to 300°F.

Combine flour, seafood seasoning, salt and pepper in a baking dish. Add the fish and shake to coat. Set aside.

Heat oil in a large skillet over medium-high heat. Add tilapia and brown on both sides, about 3 minutes per side. Place tilapia on a baking sheet that is lined with a paper grocery bag and keep warm in oven.

Add butter to pan and let it melt. Once the butter is melted, add the garlic, lemon juice, and parsley. Take the pan off the heat and pour over tilapia.

SAUTÉED EDAMAME

1	diced medium onion	$0.28
2	tbsp. canola oil	$0.06
2	tsp. chopped garlic	$0.05
1	(10-ounce) bag frozen shelled edamame, thawed	$1.40
	Kosher salt, to taste	$0.00
	Black pepper, to taste	$0.00

Heat oil in a large skillet over medium-high heat. Add onions and garlic, season with salt and pepper, and sauté for 2 minutes. Add edamame and sauté for 4 minutes until edamame are heated through and onions are tender. (Reserve leftover sautéed edamame for Round 2 Recipe: Bow Ties and Buttons, page 187.)

SERVES: 4
COOK TIME: 15 minutes
$11.11/$2.78 per person

SERVES: 4
COOK TIME: 6 minutes
$1.79/$0.45 per person

Please see Round 2 Recipe on page 187

BEEF KEBABS

3	pounds bottom round, cut into 2-inch cubes	$7.47
2	tbsp. canola oil	$0.06
1	tbsp. chopped garlic	$0.05
½	cup plain yogurt	$0.72
1	tsp. ground cumin	$0.35
2	tsp. hot sauce	$0.04
8	bamboo skewers, soaked in water	$0.08
1	large yellow onion, cut in large pieces	$0.56
	Salt, to taste	$0.00
	Black pepper, to taste	$0.00

Combine all ingredients except beef in a large bowl and mix well. Reserve half the marinade and keep in refrigerator. Add beef cubes to remaining marinade, cover and refrigerate for anywhere from 30 minutes to overnight. (Reserve 2 beef kebabs, about 6 cubes, for Round 2 Recipe, page 186.)

Preheat grill pan until smoking and spray with nonstick cooking spray.

Thread beef cubes and onion pieces onto skewers, alternating three pieces of beef and onion per skewer. Place onto grill pan and cook a couple of minutes on each side, turning once.

Serve with spicy couscous and drizzle with some of the reserved marinade. (Reserve 1/2 cup couscous and 1/4 cup marinade for Round 2 Recipe, page 186.)

SERVES: 4
COOK TIME: 8 minutes
$9.34/$2.34 per person

Please see Round 2 Recipe on page 186

SPICY COUSCOUS

1	(10-ounce) box couscous	$1.67
2	cups chicken broth	$0.99
2	tbsp. canola oil	$0.06
2	tsp. minced garlic	$0.05
1	tsp. crushed red pepper flakes	$0.08
	Kosher salt, to taste	$0.00
	Black pepper, to taste	$0.00

Heat oil in a medium saucepan. Sauté garlic with red pepper flakes while avoiding burning the garlic. Add the chicken broth and bring to a boil. Stir in couscous, cover, and take off heat. Let stand 5 minutes. Fluff with fork before serving.

SERVES: 4
COOK TIME: 10 minutes
$2.85/$0.71 per person

COCONUT CARAMEL CREAM PIE

PIE

1	premade store-brand graham cracker piecrust	$1.45
1	box (1.5-ounce) vanilla instant pudding, such as Royal	$0.33
¾	can (13.5-ounce)—about 1 cup—coconut milk (reserve ½ for caramel sauce)	$0.89
1	cup milk	$0.24
½	pint heavy cream	$1.49
3	tbsp. confectioners' sugar	$0.10
1½	tbsp. sweetened flake coconut, toasted, for garnish	$0.20

CARAMEL SAUCE

¾	cup sugar	$0.18
½	tsp. lemon juice	$0.01
½	cup coconut milk	$0.40

FOR CARAMEL SAUCE:

In a medium sauce pot combine sugar, 3 tablespoons water, and lemon juice. Heat over medium-high heat. When sugar turns amber in color, carefully and slowly whisk in coconut milk. Pour caramel into a bowl that is placed in an ice bath to cool, or transfer sauce to a bowl and place in refrigerator.

FOR PIE:

In a large bowl, whisk together the coconut milk, milk, and pudding mix. Pour half of the caramel into the bottom of the pie crust. Then pour the filling on top of the caramel.

In another large mixing bowl that has been chilled, whip the heavy cream and confectioners' sugar until stiff peaks form, but avoid its becoming dry.

Spread the whipped cream on top of the pie and refrigerate for 1 hour or until completely set. Once the pie is set, sprinkle with toasted coconut and drizzle with the remaining caramel sauce.

SERVES: 8
COOK TIME: 5 minutes
$5.29/$0.66 per person

BEEF KEBAB PITA POCKETS

2	leftover beef kebabs	**$0.00**
½	cup leftover spicy couscous	**$0.00**
¼	cup leftover	**$0.00**
	yogurt marinade	
½	cucumber, diced	**$0.50**
2	pita pockets	**$0.64**

In a small bowl, combine cucumbers and leftover reserved yogurt marinade.

Slice the top off of a pita pocket. Fill the pocket with the couscous, beef, and yogurt cucumber mixture.

SERVES: 1

$1.14 in extra ingredients

Please see Main Recipe on page 182

BOW TIES AND BUTTONS

4	slices bacon, diced	$0.68
½	box bow tie pasta	$0.60
1	cup leftover sautéed soybeans	$0.00
	Kosher salt, to taste	$0.00
	Black pepper, to taste	$0.00

Cook pasta according to package instructions.

While pasta is cooking, sauté bacon in a medium skillet over medium heat, until bacon is brown and crispy. Pour off half of the bacon fat. Add soybeans, season with salt and pepper, and sauté for two minutes.

SERVES: 4

COOK TIME: 15 minutes

$1.28 in extra ingredients

Please see Main Recipe on page 180

17. MORE THAN MEAT AND POTATOES

- Delicious light and healthy dishes designed to keep cost and calories down!
- A lot of people think they have to spend more money to eat healthier. Here are light and healthy meals that are super simple to make and won't break the bank.
- **Meal #1 total: $15.16/$3.79 per person**

  Steamed Mahi Mahi with Vegetables and Garlic Mustard Sauce, Raspberry Orange Slushie, and Ginger Green Tea
- **Meal #2 total: $13.44/$3.36 per person**

  Brown Rice and Mushroom Salad, Spicy Grilled Lemon Chicken, Raspberry Orange Slushie, and Ginger Green Tea

---

1. Steamed Mahi Mahi with Vegetables and Garlic Mustard Sauce
Total cost: $9.90/$2.48 per person

2. Brown Rice and Mushroom Salad
Total cost: $2.54/$0.64 per person

3. Spicy Grilled Lemon Chicken
Total cost: $5.64/$1.41 per person

> **MSM TIP:**
> Boneless skinless chicken breast = $4.99/lb
> Bone-in chicken breast = $2.99/lb
> Savings = $2.00 or 40%

4. Raspberry Orange Slushies
Total cost: $4.75/$1.19 per person

5. Iced Ginger Green Tea
Total cost: $0.51/$0.13 per cocktail

If you want to turn this mocktail into a true cocktail, add four ounces of prosecco for $1.56 per cocktail. Cheers!

> **MSM TIP:**
> Instant brown rice = $2.53
> Regular brown rice = $0.45
> Savings = $2.08 or 82%

6. R2R: Stuffed Peppers
$4.85 in extra ingredients

7. R2R: Grilled Chicken and Apple Wraps
$1.19 in extra ingredients

STEAMED MAHI MAHI WITH VEGETABLES AND GARLIC MUSTARD SAUCE

1	tsp. canola oil	$0.01
½	sliced red onion (reserve half for Round 2 Recipe: Grilled Chicken and Apple Wraps)	$0.34
1	medium sliced summer squash (reserve 4 pieces squash for Round 2 Recipe: Grilled Chicken and Apple Wraps)	$0.49
1	medium sliced zucchini (reserve 4 pieces zucchini for Round 2 Recipe: Grilled Chicken and Apple Wraps)	$0.49
½	(8-ounce) package sliced mushrooms	$1.00
1	cup chicken broth	$0.40
4	(4-ounce) pieces mahi mahi	$6.99
4	sprigs thyme	$0.04
1	tbsp. chopped garlic	$0.05
2	tbsp. spicy brown mustard	$0.09
	Kosher salt, to taste	$0.00
	Black pepper, to taste	$0.00

In a high-sided nonstick skillet over medium heat, add the canola oil. When it is hot, toss in the onion and cook until softened, about 5 minutes. Add the squash, zucchini, mushrooms, and broth, and season with salt and pepper. (Reserve half of raw onion, squash, and zucchini for the Round 2 Recipe: Grilled Chicken and Apple Wraps, page 196.) Season the fish with salt and pepper, place it on the vegetables, and top each piece with a sprig of thyme. Cover and steam until the fish is cooked through, about 10 minutes.

Remove the fish to a plate and cover to keep warm. Remove the vegetables with a slotted spoon and keep warm. Turn the heat to high, add the garlic to the pan juices, and cook for 30 seconds. Whisk in the mustard and cook until the sauce reduces and thickens, about 2–3 minutes. Taste, and season with more salt and pepper, if needed.

Spoon the vegetables onto four plates, and top each with a piece of fish. Pour the sauce over the fish and serve.

SERVES: 4
COOK TIME: 20 minutes
$9.90/$2.48 per person

Please see Round 2 Recipe on page 196

BROWN RICE AND MUSHROOM SALAD

1	cup chicken broth	$0.40
2	cups brown rice	$0.45
½	chopped red onion	$0.34
2	chopped stalks celery	$0.30
1	medium shredded carrot	$0.16
1	tsp. black pepper	$0.00
½	(8-ounce) package sliced mushrooms, chopped	$1.00
1	tbsp. chopped fresh parsley	$0.02
1	tsp. chopped fresh thyme	$0.01
	Reserved juice of 2 lemons (page 192)	$0.00
1	tbsp. Dijon mustard	$0.09
1	tbsp. canola oil	$0.00
1	tsp. kosher salt, plus more to taste	$0.00
	Black pepper, to taste	$0.00

In a saucepan over high heat, add 2 cups water, chicken broth, and 1 teaspoon salt. Stir in rice and bring to a boil. Reduce the heat to low, cover, and simmer until the rice is tender, about 40–45 minutes. Fluff the rice with a fork and spread it out onto a sheet pan to cool.

In a large bowl, add the onion, celery, carrot, pepper, mushrooms, parsley, thyme, and the cooled rice. Gently mix everything together (reserve 1½ cups for the Round 2 Recipe: Stuffed Peppers, page 196). In a medium bowl, whisk together the lemon juice, Dijon mustard, and salt and pepper to taste. Whisk in the oil. Pour the dressing over the salad and gently toss everything together. Refrigerate unless serving right away.

SERVES: 4
COOK TIME: 45 minutes
$2.54/$0.64 per person

Please see Round 2 Recipe on page 196

SPICY GRILLED LEMON CHICKEN

1½	pounds bone-in chicken breast (reserve tenders for Round 2 Recipe, page 196)	$4.49
1	tbsp. canola oil	$0.03
	Zest of 2 lemons (reserve juice for Brown Rice and Mushroom Salad, page 194)	$1.00
1	tsp. red pepper flakes	$0.08
1	tbsp. chopped fresh parsley	$0.02
1	tbsp. chopped fresh thyme	$0.02
	Kosher salt, to taste	$0.00
	Black pepper, to taste	$0.00

Remove the skin and bones from the chicken breasts and separate out the tenders. Cut the breasts in half horizontally, put the chicken between two pieces of plastic wrap, and pound them thin with a rolling pin or small skillet.

Pour the oil into a resealable plastic bag and add the lemon zest, red pepper flakes, parsley, thyme, and pepper. Mix it all together and add the chicken breasts and tenders. Seal the bag, put it in a bowl, and refrigerate for at least 2 hours.

When you are ready to cook, remove the chicken from the refrigerator and let it come to room temperature while you heat the grill. Put the chicken breasts and tenders on the grill, season them with salt, and cook through, about 4–5 minutes on each side.

Serve the breasts while hot, with the Brown Rice and Mushroom Salad. (Reserve the tenders for Round 2 Recipe: Grilled Chicken and Apple Wraps, page 196.)

TIP: *Slicing the chicken breasts in half will make pounding much easier and will also help ensure they cook through on the grill without drying out from overcooking.*

SERVES: 4
COOK TIME: 10 minutes
$5.64/$1.41 per person

Please see Round 2 Recipe on page 196

RASPBERRY ORANGE SLUSHIES

1	cup orange juice	$0.24
1	(12-ounce) package frozen raspberries	$4.50
1	tbsp. sugar	$0.01

Pour the orange juice into an ice cube tray and freeze.

Put the raspberries into the bowl of a food processor. Add the frozen orange juice cubes and the sugar. Process until the mixture is the texture of snow, about 45–60 seconds. Serve immediately, or transfer to a freezer container and freeze for later.

SERVES: 4
$4.75/$1.19 per person

ICED GINGER GREEN TEA

4	green tea bags	$0.16
½	cup sugar	$0.10
1	1-inch piece ginger, sliced	$0.25
4	ounces prosecco, optional	$2.35

Put four green tea bags into a heatproof container and pour over 1 quart boiling water. Let steep until it comes to room temperature, about 1 hour. Remove the tea bags and discard. While the tea is steeping, in a saucepan over medium-high heat, bring 1 cup water, the sugar, and ginger to a boil. Stir to dissolve the sugar, remove from the heat, and allow to cool to room temperature, about 1 hour. Store the tea and ginger simple syrup in the refrigerator until ready to serve.

To serve, fill glasses with ice and pour in the tea. Sweeten to taste with the ginger simple syrup. Garnish with a slice of ginger. For the adults, top with 1 ounce of prosecco.

SERVES: 4
COOK TIME: 5 minutes
$0.51/$0.13 per person

STUFFED PEPPERS

2	red bell peppers	**$3.36**
	Reserved brown rice mixture	**$0.00**
	(page 191)	
1	(15-ounce) can diced	**$0.99**
	tomatoes, drained	
½	cup shredded mozzarella	**$0.50**

Heat the oven to 350°F.

Cut the red peppers in half and scoop out the seeds and ribs. Place them onto a baking sheet.

To the reserved brown rice mixture, stir in the tomato and ⅔ of the cheese. Stuff the peppers with the rice mixture, dividing it evenly. Top the peppers with the remaining cheese. Bake at 350°F for 25–30 minutes or until the pepper is tender and the cheese has melted.

> **SERVES:** 4
> **COOK TIME:** 30 minutes
> **$4.85 in extra ingredients**

Please see Main Recipe on page 191

GRILLED CHICKEN AND APPLE WRAPS

	Reserved chicken (page 192)	**$0.00**
	Reserved vegetables	**$0.00**
	(page 190)	
1	apple, peeled and chopped	**$0.36**
2	tbsp. low-fat mayonnaise	**$0.06**
2	tsp. spicy brown mustard	**$0.03**
1	tbsp. chopped fresh parsley	**$0.02**
4	flour tortillas	**$0.72**
	Kosher salt, to taste	**$0.00**
	Black pepper, to taste	**$0.00**

Chop the reserved chicken and vegetables and mix them all together with the apple. In a small bowl, whisk together the mayonnaise, mustard, parsley, and salt and pepper to taste.

Toss with the chopped chicken mixture. Divide the mixture among the tortillas, wrap up, and enjoy.

> **SERVES:** 4
> **$1.19 in extra ingredients**

Please see Main Recipes on pages 190 and 192

18. PERFECT PASTA PLATES

- Delicious pasta dishes guaranteed to put an "al dente" in your budget.
- You can make any of these three wonderful pasta dishes (with a drink) for under $3.00 per person
- **Meal #1 total: $11.38/$2.85 per person**
  Pork Ragu over Penne and Orange Basil Bellinis
- **Meal #2 total: $5.43/$1.36 per person**
  Spaghetti Carbonara and Orange Basil Bellinis
- **Meal #3 total: $5.54/$1.38 per person**
  Spaghetti with Clam Sauce and Orange Basil Bellinis

1. Pork Ragu over Penne
Total cost: $10.19/$2.55 per person

2. Spaghetti Carbonara
Total cost: $4.24/$1.06 per person

3. Orange Basil Bellinis
Total cost: $1.19/$0.30 per glass

4. Spaghetti with Clam Sauce
Total cost: $4.35/$1.09 per person

5. R2R: Lasagna Roll-Ups
$3.56 in extra ingredients

6. R2R: Savory Noodle Pie
$3.41 in extra ingredients

MSM TIP:
Beef vs. Pork comparison
Beef bone-in chuck roast
= $2.99/lb
Bone-in pork shoulder roast
= $1.69/lb
Savings = $1.30 or 43%

MSM TIP:
Bacon vs. Pancetta
Pancetta = $10.49/lb
Bacon = $3.49/lb
Savings = $7.00 or 67%

MSM TIP:
Substitute 4 ounces of
prosecco for the sparkling
water for $1.56 per cocktail

MSM TIP:
Fresh clams (10 ounces) =
$4.60
Whole canned clams (10
ounces) = $2.09
Savings = $2.51 or 55%

PORK RAGU OVER PENNE

1	tbsp. canola oil	$0.03
1	(4-pound) bone-in pork butt shoulder roast	$6.76
1	medium chopped yellow onion	$0.28
2	chopped carrots	$0.32
2	chopped stalks celery	$0.30
1	tbsp. chopped garlic	$0.05
1	(28-ounce) can chopped tomatoes	$0.99
1	tbsp. chopped fresh basil, plus more for garnish	$0.02
1	(16-ounce) package penne	$1.29
2	tbsp. Parmesan, for garnish	$0.15
½	can tomato paste	$0.25
	Kosher salt, to taste	$0.00
	Black pepper, to taste	$0.00

Heat a large skillet over medium-high heat with 1 tablespoon canola oil. Season the pork butt with salt and pepper, and brown it on all sides, about 10–15 minutes. While the pork is browning, to the bowl of a slow cooker add the onion, carrots, and celery, and season them with salt and pepper. Put the pork on top of the vegetables and add the garlic and tomatoes. Cook the pork on low for 6–8 hours. When it is done, remove the pork. Add the basil and the tomato paste to the vegetables, and stir to incorporate. Shred the pork and add it to the vegetables. Let this simmer, uncovered, while you cook the pasta. (Save 2 cups of the ragu for the Round 2 Recipe: Lasagna Roll-Ups, page 206.)

Bring a large pot of salted water to a boil. Add the penne, stir, and cover the pot. When it returns to the boil, remove the cover and stir it again. Cook until the pasta is al dente, about 8 minutes. Reserve 1 cup of the pasta cooking water and drain the pasta. (Save 1 cup of the pasta for the Round 2 Recipe: Savory Noodle Pie, page 208.) Put the pasta back into the pot, stir in the ragu, and put the pot over medium heat. Add some of the cooking water if the sauce is too thick. Cook for a minute or two, so the pasta absorbs the flavors of the sauce. Serve immediately, garnished with Parmesan and basil leaves.

SERVES: 4
COOK TIME: 8 hours
$10.19/$2.55 per person

Please see Round 2 Recipes on pages 206 and 208

SPAGHETTI CARBONARA

1	(16-ounce) package spaghetti	**$1.29**
8	strips bacon	**$1.36**
1	tbsp. chopped garlic	**$0.05**
4	large eggs	**$0.44**
½	cup Parmesan cheese	**$1.08**
1	tbsp. chopped fresh parsley	**$0.02**
	Kosher salt, to taste	**$0.00**

Bring a large pot of salted water to a boil. Add the spaghetti, cover the pot, and bring it back to a boil. Remove the cover, stir, and cook until al dente, about 8 minutes. Reserve 1 cup of the pasta cooking water. Drain the pasta and set aside. (Reserve 1 cup of pasta for the Round 2 Recipe: Savory Noodle Pie, page 208.)

While the pasta is cooking, place 8 strips of bacon into a large skillet over medium heat, and cook until they are crispy. Drain the bacon (reserve 2 strips for the Round 2 Recipe: Savory Noodle Pie, page 208), chop it, and set aside. Remove all but 1 tablespoon of fat from the pan, add the garlic and cook for 30 seconds. Add the cooked spaghetti and toss to coat with the garlic and fat. Turn off the heat, and add the beaten eggs and half the cheese. Toss gently to coat the pasta and cook the eggs. Toss in the chopped bacon. Add some pasta water if the sauce is too thick. Serve immediately, garnished with the remaining cheese and parsley.

SERVES: 4
COOK TIME: 20 minutes
$4.24/$1.06 per person

Please see Round 2 Recipe on page 208

ORANGE BASIL BELLINIS

1	cup sugar	$0.20
½	cup basil leaves	$0.16
	Juice of 1 orange	$0.50
1	(33-ounce) bottle sparkling water or seltzer	$0.33
1	bottle prosecco, optional	$9.95

In a small saucepan over medium-high heat, add the water and sugar and bring to a boil, stirring to dissolve the sugar. Remove from the heat, add the basil, and let cool. Strain out the basil and refrigerate.

Pour 1 tablespoon of orange juice and 1 tablespoon basil simple syrup into a champagne flute. Top with sparkling water and garnish with a slice of orange and a basil leaf. For the adults, substitute prosecco for the sparkling water.

SERVES: 4
COOK TIME: 5 minutes
$1.19/$0.30 per person

SPAGHETTI WITH CLAM SAUCE

1	(16-ounce) package spaghetti	$1.29
1	tbsp. canola oil	$0.03
1	tbsp. chopped garlic	$0.05
1	cup canned chopped tomatoes	$0.25
1	(10-ounce) can whole clams	$2.09
	Juice of 1 lemon (save zest for Round 2 Recipe, page 206)	$0.50
2	tbsp. unsalted butter	$0.12
1	tbsp. chopped fresh parsley	$0.02
	Kosher salt, to taste	$0.00
	Black pepper, to taste	$0.00

Bring a large pot of salted water to a boil. Add the spaghetti, cover the pot, and bring back to a boil. Remove the cover, stir, and cook until al dente, about 8 minutes. Reserve 1 cup of the pasta cooking water. Drain the pasta and set aside. (Reserve 1 cup of pasta for the Round 2 Recipe: Savory Noodle Pie, page 208.)

Heat a large skillet over medium heat with the oil. Add the garlic and tomatoes and cook for 30 seconds. Add the clams with their juices and the lemon juice. Cook for 2 minutes. Add the spaghetti and cook for another 2 minutes. Add the butter and stir. Pour in some of the pasta cooking water if the pasta is too dry. Remove from the heat and stir in the parsley and black pepper. Serve immediately.

SERVES: 4
COOK TIME: 12 minutes
$4.35/$1.09 per person

Please see Round 2 Recipes on pages 206 and 208

LASAGNA ROLL-UPS

	Nonstick cooking spray	$0.00
½	(16-ounce) box lasagna noodles, or 8 noodles	$0.75
	Reserved Pork Ragu (page 200)	$0.00
1	(15-ounce) container ricotta cheese	$2.29
	Reserved lemon zest (page 204)	$0.00
1	tbsp. chopped fresh sage	$0.02
½	cup shredded mozzarella	$0.50
	Kosher salt, to taste	$0.00

Heat oven to 350°F. Spray a baking dish large enough to hold 8 rolls with cooking spray.

Bring a large pot of salted water to a boil. Add the lasagna, cover the pot, and bring it back to a boil. Remove the cover, stir, and cook until al dente, about 8 minutes. Reserve 1 cup of the pasta cooking water. Drain the pasta and set aside.

In a saucepan over medium heat, add the Pork Ragu and ½ cup of the reserved pasta cooking water, and warm it through. (Add more water if it is too thick.) Put the ricotta into a bowl and stir in the zest and sage.

Spread a thin layer of the sauce in the bottom of the prepared baking dish. Put a lasagna noodle on your work surface and spread ¼ cup of the ricotta mixture onto it, leaving the 2 inches on one end clear. Top the cheese with ¼ cup of the ragu and roll up the noodle, starting from the loaded end. Place it into the baking dish and continue with the remaining noodles, ricotta, and ragu. Spread any remaining ragu over the top of the rolls, and sprinkle with mozzarella cheese. Put the pan onto a baking sheet and bake until the cheese is bubbling and browned, about 30–35 minutes. Let rest 10–15 minutes before serving.

SERVES: 4
COOK TIME: 45 minutes
$3.56 in extra ingredients

Please see Main Recipes on pages 200 and 204

SAVORY NOODLE PIE

	Nonstick cooking spray	$0.00
	Reserved 3 cups pasta (pages 200, 202, 204)	$0.00
1	cup shredded mozzarella	$1.00
3	chopped scallions	$0.39
	Reserved chopped bacon (page 202)	$0.00
2	large eggs	$0.22
½	cup milk	$0.08
¼	cup Parmesan cheese	$0.59
1	(14.5-ounce) can chopped tomatoes, drained	$0.99
1	tbsp. extra virgin olive oil	$0.12
1	tbsp. chopped fresh basil	$0.02
	Kosher salt, to taste	$0.00
	Black pepper, to taste	$0.00

Heat oven to 350°F. Spray a 9-inch pie dish with cooking spray.

Mix the reserved pastas together with half the mozzarella, scallions, and the reserved bacon. Pat the pasta mixture into the pie dish. Whisk the eggs with the milk, half the Parmesan cheese, and salt and pepper to taste. Pour egg mixture over the pasta and sprinkle with the remaining mozzarella and Parmesan cheese. Place dish on a baking sheet and bake until set and the top is browned and bubbling, about 30–35 minutes. Allow to rest for 15 minutes before serving.

While the pie is baking, make the sauce: Combine the tomatoes, olive oil, basil, and salt and pepper to taste. Spoon the sauce over slices of the Noodle Pie.

TIP: *Tossing the eggs in the heated pan will help to cook the eggs, and will also keep them from scrambling, resulting in a creamy delicious sauce.*

SERVES: 4
COOK TIME: 35 minutes
$3.41 in extra ingredients

Please see Main Recipes on pages 200, 202, and 204

19. FROM THE MEDITERRANEAN

- A Mediterranean menu at a price that will float your boat!
- Mediterranean food is really something special. It's a combination of fresh produce, fantastic spices, and a handful of simple ingredients, which also makes it the perfect candidate for delicious money saving meals.
- **Meal #1 total: $10.72/$2.68 per person**
  Moussaka, Walnut Raisin Tarts, and Rosemary Lemon Spritzer
- **Meal #2 total: $9.61/$2.40 per person**
  Spinach and Pasta Pie, Walnut Raisin Tarts, and Rosemary Lemon Spritzer

---

1. Moussaka
Total cost: $6.82/$1.14 per person

2. Spinach and Pasta Pie
Total cost: $5.71/$1.43 per person

3. Walnut Raisin Tarts
Total cost: $2.95/$0.25 per person

> **TIP:** *Transforming the muffin tin you already have into a tart pan saves megabucks, and you can still bake like a pro.*

MSM TIP:
Refrigerator pie dough = $3.29
Box mix = $0.89
Savings = $2.40 or 73%

4. Rosemary Lemon Spritzer
Total cost: $0.95/$0.24 per person

> *If you want to turn these mocktails into true cocktails, add an ounce of gin for another $0.47 per cocktail. Cheers!*

5. R2R: Spinach and Mushroom Pasta
$3.45 in extra ingredients

6. R2R: Eggplant Dip
$1.46 in extra ingredients

MOUSSAKA

2	tbsp. canola oil	$0.06
2	eggplants, cut lengthwise into ¼-inch slices	$2.08
1	medium chopped yellow onion	$0.28
1	tbsp. chopped garlic	$0.05
1	pound (80% lean) ground beef	$2.19
2	tsp. Italian seasoning	$0.12
1	tsp. cinnamon	$0.09
1	(28-ounce) can crushed tomatoes	$0.99
2	tbsp. butter	$0.12
2	tbsp. flour	$0.02
1½	cups milk	$0.24
¼	cup grated Parmesan cheese	$0.54
2	tbsp. chopped fresh parsley	$0.04
	Kosher salt, to taste	$0.00
	Black pepper, to taste	$0.00

SERVES: 6
COOK TIME: 1 hour 10 minutes
$6.82/$1.14 per person

Preheat the oven to 375°F. Brush a 9 × 9-inch baking dish with a little oil.

Put the eggplant slices in a single layer on a baking sheet. Brush both sides with oil and season with salt and pepper. Bake until browned and softened, about 10–15 minutes.

In a large skillet over medium-high heat, cook the beef, breaking up the pieces with a wooden spoon, until it is cooked through, about 8–10 minutes. Remove the meat from the pan and strain to drain off excess fat. Remove all but 1 tablespoon of fat from the pan, add the onions, and cook until they soften, about 5 minutes. Add the garlic and cook for 30 seconds. Return the meat to the pan, add the Italian seasoning, ½ teaspoon cinnamon, and salt and pepper to taste. Stir in the tomatoes and simmer until thick and the flavors have combined, about 20–25 minutes. Taste, and adjust seasoning with salt and pepper.

In a small saucepan over medium heat, melt the butter. Whisk in the flour and cook for 2 minutes. Slowly whisk in the milk, bring to a simmer, and cook until béchamel sauce is very thick. Add the remaining ½ teaspoon cinnamon to the béchamel and season with salt and pepper.

Put a layer of eggplant into the baking dish. Spread the beef mixture evenly over the top. Put another layer of eggplant on top. (Reserve remaining eggplant for Round 2 Recipe: Eggplant Dip, page 219.) Pour the béchamel sauce over the top and sprinkle with the cheese.

Bake until browned and bubbling, about 25–30 minutes. Remove from the oven and let it rest for 15 minutes. Garnish with the parsley before serving.

Please see Round 2 Recipe on page 219

SPINACH AND PASTA PIE

3	large eggs	$0.33
2	tbsp. canola oil	$0.06
1	(16-ounce) box spaghetti, cooked according to package directions, and drained	$1.29
1	medium chopped yellow onion (reserve half for Round 2 Recipe, page 218)	$0.28
2	tsp. chopped garlic	$0.03
¼	cup milk	$0.08
2	tsp. Italian seasoning	$0.12
½	(4-ounce) package crumbled feta cheese	$1.25
2	(10-ounce) packages frozen chopped spinach, thawed and drained (reserve ¾ cup for Round 2 Recipe, page 218)	$0.98
1	plum tomato, sliced thin	$0.75
¼	cup Parmesan cheese	$0.54
	Kosher salt, to taste	$0.00
	Black pepper, to taste	$0.00

Preheat the oven to 350°F.

In a large bowl, beat together 1 egg with 1 tablespoon oil, and season with salt and pepper. Add half the spaghetti (reserve half for Round 2 Recipe: Spinach and Mushroom Pasta, page 218). Toss well to coat, and press into a 9-inch deep-dish pie pan to form a crust.

In a skillet over medium-high heat, add the remaining oil. When it is hot, add the onion and cook until it is softened, about 5 minutes. Add the garlic and cook for 30 seconds. Remove from the heat and cool to room temperature.

In a large bowl, whisk together the remaining 2 eggs, milk, Italian seasoning, and salt and pepper to taste. Stir in the cheese, spinach (reserve ¾ cup for Round 2 Recipe: Spinach and Mushroom Pasta, page 218), and cooled onions. Pour mixture on top of the spaghetti piecrust. Top with tomato slices and sprinkle with Parmesan cheese. Put pan onto a baking sheet and bake until the pie is set and golden brown, about 35–40 minutes. Remove and let rest for 15 minutes before slicing.

SERVES: 4
COOK TIME: 45 minutes
$5.71/$1.43 per person

Please see Round 2 Recipe on page 218

WALNUT RAISIN TARTS

	Ingredient	Cost
	Nonstick cooking spray	$0.00
1	box piecrust mix, prepared according to package directions	$0.89
3	tbsp. unsalted butter, at room temperature	$0.18
⅓	cup packed brown sugar	$0.12
2	large eggs, at room temperature	$0.22
½	tsp. vanilla extract	$0.22
½	tsp. pumpkin pie spice	$0.15
½	cup raisins, roughly chopped	$0.32
½	cup walnuts, roughly chopped	$0.85

Preheat the oven to 375°F. Spray a 12-cup muffin tin with nonstick cooking spray.

Divide the pie dough into 12 pieces and press them evenly into the bottoms and up the sides of the muffin cups to form crusts.

In a medium bowl with an electric hand mixer, beat together the butter and sugar until fluffy. Add the eggs, vanilla, and spice and mix well. Stir in the raisins and walnuts. Spoon the mixture, dividing it evenly, into the crusts.

Put the muffin tin on a baking sheet and bake until the filling is set, about 18–20 minutes. Remove the pan from the oven and allow to cool for 10 minutes. Carefully unmold the tarts, put them onto a rack, and let them cool to room temperature.

SERVES: 12
COOK TIME: 12 minutes
$2.95/$0.25 per person

ROSEMARY LEMON SPRITZER

½	cup sugar	$0.10
1	sprig rosemary, plus more for garnish	$0.02
1	lemon	$0.50
1	liter bottle sparkling water	$0.33
4	ounces ouzo or gin	$1.88

Zest the lemon. Cut four thin slices out of the middle of the lemon and reserve for garnish. Squeeze out the juice from the ends and set aside.

In a small pan over medium-high heat, stir together the sugar with ½ cup of water until the sugar dissolves. Bring to a boil, remove from the heat, and add the rosemary sprig and lemon zest. Let cool to room temperature, strain into a clean jar, and refrigerate until ready to use, or up to two weeks.

Fill four glasses with ice, pour 2 tablespoons of the flavored syrup into each, add a little lemon juice, and fill with sparkling water. Top with ouzo or gin, if using. Garnish with a lemon slice and a small sprig of rosemary.

SERVES: 4
COOK TIME: 5 minutes
$0.95/$0.24 PER PERSON

SPINACH AND MUSHROOM PASTA

1	tbsp. canola oil	**$0.03**
	Reserved ½ medium chopped onion (page 213)	**$0.00**
1	(10-ounce) package sliced baby portobello mushrooms	**$2.49**
1	tbsp. chopped garlic	**$0.05**
2	tsp. Italian seasoning	**$0.12**
¼	tsp. red pepper flakes	**$0.02**
	Reserved spinach, drained well (page 213)	**$0.00**
	Reserved pasta (page 213)	**$0.00**
1	tbsp. olive oil	**$0.12**
¼	cup grated Parmesan cheese	**$0.54**
¼	cup fresh chopped basil	**$0.08**
	Kosher salt, to taste	**$0.00**
	Black pepper, to taste	**$0.00**

In a large skillet over medium heat, add the canola oil. When it is hot, add the onions and cook until they are soft, about 5 minutes. Add the mushrooms, season with salt and pepper, and cook until they are lightly browned and have given up their liquid, about 5 minutes. Add the garlic, Italian seasoning, and red pepper flakes, and cook for 1 minute. Stir in the spinach and cook until warmed through, about 5 minutes. Toss in the pasta and cook until warmed through, about 2 minutes. Remove from the heat and stir in the olive oil, cheese, and basil. Serve immediately.

SERVES: 2

COOK TIME: 20 minutes

$3.45 in extra ingredients

Please see Main Recipe on page 213

EGGPLANT DIP

1	small head of garlic	$0.70
1	tsp. canola oil	$0.01
	Reserved eggplant (page 212)	$0.00
¼	cup roughly chopped fresh parsley	$0.08
½	tsp. cumin	$0.06
1	tbsp. lemon juice	$0.00
3	tbsp. olive oil	$0.08
¼	tsp. paprika	$0.02
3	pita pockets, cut into quarters and toasted	$0.51
	Kosher salt, to taste	$0.00
	Black pepper, to taste	$0.00

Preheat the oven to 400°F.

Slice off the pointed top of the garlic head and put it on a square of aluminum foil, cut-side up. Drizzle with the canola oil and season with salt and pepper. Wrap it up, place it on a baking sheet, and bake until the garlic is soft, about 45 minutes. Unwrap and let cool for a bit.

Into the bowl of a food processor, squeeze in the garlic. Add the eggplant, parsley, cumin, and lemon juice, and pulse to combine. With the processor running, drizzle in the olive oil. Taste, and adjust the seasoning with salt and pepper. Scoop the dip into a bowl, sprinkle with paprika, and serve with the toasted pita.

SERVES: 4

COOK TIME: 45 minutes

$1.46 in extra ingredients

Please see Main Recipe on page 212

20. MINUTE MEAL MAGIC

- Save money *and* time with delicious dishes that go from the kitchen to the plate in the blink of an eye.
- **Meal #1 total: $16.28/$4.07 per person**

    Shrimp Scampi, a Banana Daiquiri, and a S'mores Pudding Parfait
- **Meal #2 total: $12.50/$3.13 per person**

    Steak and Cheese Hoagies, a Banana Daiquiri, and a S'mores Pudding Parfait

---

1. Shrimp Scampi over Pesto Couscous

Total cost: $10.97/$2.74 per person

Buying the same-sized package of smaller-sized shrimp leaves you with more individual pieces to eat, and in addition, shrimp decrease in price as they decrease in size

2. Steak and Cheese Hoagies

Total cost: $7.19/$1.80 per person

3. Banana Daiquiri

Total cost: $1.91/$0.48 per person

Turn mocktail into cocktail by adding an ounce of white rum for $0.43

4. S'mores Pudding Parfait

Total cost: $3.40/$0.85 per person

TIP: *Instant pudding costs the same as making pudding from scratch, and it saves you time.*

5. R2R: Shrimp Bruschetta

$1.92 in extra ingredients

6. R2R: Couscous Stuffed Tomatoes

$2.52 in extra ingredients

MSM TIP:

Frozen shrimp 26-30 ct (jumbo) = $10.49/lb
Frozen shrimp 51-60 ct (medium) = $6.49/lb
Savings = $4.00 or 38%

SHRIMP SCAMPI OVER PESTO COUSCOUS

1	cup fresh basil leaves	$0.32
2	tbsp. chopped garlic	$0.10
¼	cup chopped walnuts	$0.84
¼	cup grated Parmesan cheese	$0.58
⅓	cup, plus 1 tbsp. canola oil	$0.19
1	(10-ounce) package couscous	$1.69
½	tsp. red pepper flakes	$0.04
½	cup chicken broth	$0.20
	Juice of 1 lemon	$0.50
1	(1-pound) bag frozen raw shrimp, thawed, shelled, deveined, tails left on	$6.49
1	tbsp. chopped fresh parsley	$0.02
	Kosher salt, to taste	$0.00
	Black pepper, to taste	$0.00

Make the pesto: In the bowl of a food processor, pulse together the basil, 1 tablespoon garlic, walnuts, and Parmesan cheese. With the food processor running, slowly drizzle in ⅓ cup oil. Season with salt and pepper.

Make the couscous: In a medium saucepan over medium-high heat, bring 2 cups of water and ½ teaspoon of salt to a boil. Remove from the heat, stir in the couscous, cover, and let stand for 5 minutes, or while you cook the shrimp. (Reserve 1 cup couscous for Round 2 Recipe: Couscous Stuffed Tomatoes, page 228.) When you are ready to serve, stir half the pesto into the couscous. (Reserve the remaining pesto for Round 2 Recipe: Shrimp Bruschetta, page 228.)

Cook the shrimp: In a large skillet over medium heat, add 1 tablespoon oil, 1 tablespoon garlic, and red pepper flakes, and cook for 30 seconds. Add the broth and lemon juice, and cook until it bubbles. Add the shrimp, season with salt and pepper, give it a good stir, and cook until the shrimp is pink and cooked through, about 3–4 minutes. Remove the pan from the heat and stir in the parsley. (Save 4 shrimp for Round 2 Recipe: Shrimp Bruschetta, page 228.) Serve immediately, spooning the shrimp and sauce over the Pesto Couscous.

SERVES: 4
COOK TIME: 10 minutes
$10.97/$2.74 per person

Please see Round 2 Recipe on page 228

STEAK AND CHEESE HOAGIES

2	tbsp. Worcestershire sauce	$0.12
1	tbsp. soy sauce	$0.09
1	tbsp. spicy brown mustard	$0.05
1	tsp. chopped fresh rosemary	$0.02
½	tsp. red pepper flakes	$0.04
1½	pounds top round steak	$4.04
	Nonstick cooking spray	$0.00
4	hero rolls	$2.26
1¼	cups shredded Monterey Jack cheese (reserve ¼ cup for Round 2 Recipe, page 228)	$0.28
½	cup mayonnaise	$0.23
1	tbsp. hot sauce	$0.06
	Kosher salt, to taste	$0.00
	Black pepper, to taste	$0.00

Heat the grill and the broiler.

In a large bowl, whisk together the Worcestershire sauce, soy sauce, mustard, rosemary, and red pepper flakes. Set aside.

Season the steak with salt and pepper. Spray the grill with nonstick spray. Grill the meat until it is medium-rare, about 2 minutes per side. Remove the steak from the grill, cover it with foil, and allow it to rest for 5 minutes. Slice the steak thinly and toss the slices in the marinade.

(Reserve ¼ cup of the cheese for the Round 2 Recipe: Couscous Stuffed Tomatoes, page 228.) Cut the rolls in half, sprinkle 2 tablespoons of the cheese evenly over each piece of bread, and put them under the broiler until the cheese is melted and bubbling, about 1–2 minutes.

In a small bowl, whisk together the mayonnaise and hot sauce.

(Reserve 4 pieces of beef for the Round 2 Recipe: Couscous Stuffed Tomatoes, page 228.) Put one quarter of the beef on each of the roll bottom-halves. Spread a quarter of the spiced mayonnaise on top of the meat, and cover with the top of the roll. Cut in half and serve.

TIP: *Monterey Jack cheese is milder than some other cheeses, like sharp yellow Cheddar or Gruyère, so its flavor meshes perfectly with the spicy mayo that is included in this recipe.*

Please see Round 2 Recipe on page 228

SERVES: 4
COOK TIME: 6 minutes
$7.19/$1.80 per person

BANANA DAIQUIRI

2	large bananas, sliced	$0.60
1	cup coconut milk	$0.88
	Juice of 1 lime	$0.33
½	cup sugar	$0.10
4	cups ice	$0.00
	White rum, optional	$1.70

In a blender, add 1 banana, ½ cup coconut milk, juice of ½ lime, ¼ cup sugar, and 2 cups of ice. Blend until smooth, about 1–2 minutes. Pour into two tall glasses and stir in 1 ounce of white rum each for the adults. Repeat for two more drinks.

SERVES: 4
$1.91/$0.48 per person

S'MORES PUDDING PARFAIT

1	(5.9-ounce) box chocolate instant pudding	$1.49
3	cups milk	$0.48
⅓	(14.4-ounce) box graham crackers, or 9 boards	$0.66
1	(10.5-ounce) bag mini marshmallows	$0.77

Make the pudding according to package directions. Have four parfait or wineglasses ready.

Put a layer of pudding in the bottom of each glass. Crumble on some graham crackers and then a handful of marshmallows. Repeat two more times, ending with the marshmallows. Carefully light a kitchen torch and lightly brown the top layer of marshmallows.

SERVES: 4
$3.40/$0.85 per person

SHRIMP BRUSCHETTA

2	baguettes	$1.14
	Reserved shrimp from	$0.00
	Shrimp Scampi,	
	chopped (page 222)	
2	Roma tomatoes, chopped	$0.78
	Reserved pesto (page 222)	$0.00
	Kosher salt, to taste	$0.00
	Black pepper, to taste	$0.00

Heat the oven to 350°F.

Slice the baguette into ¼-inch pieces on the diagonal. Put them onto a baking sheet and bake, turning once, until they are golden brown on both sides, about 10 minutes.

In a bowl, combine the shrimp, tomato, pesto, and salt and pepper to taste. Spread a tablespoon of the mixture onto each piece of bread and serve.

> **SERVES:** 4
> **COOK TIME:** 10 minutes
> **$1.92 in extra ingredients**

Please see Main Recipe on page 222

COUSCOUS STUFFED TOMATOES

2	beefsteak tomatoes	$2.50
	Reserved steak (page 224)	$0.00
	Reserved couscous (page 222)	$0.00
1	tbsp. chopped fresh parsley	$0.02
	Reserved cheese (page 224)	$0.00

Heat the broiler.

Cut the tomatoes in half across their equator. Scoop out the insides to form shell. Chop pulp, and put it into a bowl. Chop the reserved steak and add it to the bowl. Add the couscous and chopped parsley and mix it all together. Stuff each tomato half with the couscous mixture and place on a baking sheet. Sprinkle a tablespoon of cheese onto each tomato. Broil until the cheese is melted and bubbling, about 1–2 minutes.

> **SERVES:** 4
> **COOK TIME:** 2 minutes
> **$2.52 in extra ingredients**

Please see Main Recipes on pages 222 and 224

21. GOING GLOBAL WITH THAI

- Put that takeout menu away! Here are all your Thai favorites—make them at home and you save a bundle.
- These Thai meals don't just save you a lot of money over takeout. In general, these will be 40–50 percent cheaper than buying prepackaged Thai meals at the grocery store.
- If you were to have the same dinner at a Thai restaurant, it would cost you $74.00, and that doesn't include the tip.
- **Meal total: $15.44/$3.86 per person**
  Basil Chicken, Pad Thai, Rice Pudding with
  Coconut Milk, and Thai Iced Tea

---

1. Basil Chicken
Total cost: $8.95/$2.24 per person

2. Pad Thai
Total cost: $7.08/$1.77 per person

3. Rice Pudding with Coconut Milk
Total cost: $4.55/$1.14 per person

4. Thai Iced Tea
Total cost: $1.94/$0.49 per person

5. R2R: Coconut Chicken Soup
$0.52 in extra ingredients

6. R2R: Summer Rolls
$1.85 in extra ingredients

BASIL CHICKEN

3	cups white rice	$0.90
1	(4-pound) whole chicken, cut into parts	$6.76
2	tbsp. canola oil	$0.06
1	medium sliced yellow onion	$0.28
1	tbsp. chopped garlic	$0.05
1	small serrano chili pepper, sliced in half	$0.29
2	tsp. fish sauce	$0.13
2	tsp. brown sugar	$0.01
2	tsp. low-sodium soy sauce	$0.06
1	cup fresh basil leaves	$0.32
1	tbsp. lime juice	$0.09

Put the rice into a medium pot and pour in 6 cups of cold water. Put the pot over medium-high heat, cover, and bring to a boil. Reduce the heat to a simmer and cook until the water is absorbed, about 30 minutes. (Reserve 2 cups cooked rice for Rice Pudding with Coconut Milk, page 235.)

Remove the chicken breasts from the bone, keeping skin. Slice into ½-inch strips and cut each strip into 2-inch pieces. (Reserve the bones and remaining chicken for Round 2 Recipe: Coconut Chicken Soup, page 237.) In a large wok or skillet over high heat, add the oil. When the oil is hot, add the chicken and stir-fry until it is almost completely cooked through, about 5 minutes. Add the onions and cook until lightly browned. Add the garlic and chili and cook 1 minute. Stir in the fish sauce, sugar, soy sauce, and 2 tablespoons of water, and cook 1 minute more. Add the basil and remove from the heat once it has wilted. Stir in the lime juice and serve over rice.

SERVES: 4
COOK TIME: 15 minutes
$8.95/$2.24 per person

Please see Round 2 Recipe on page 237

PAD THAI

1	(16-ounce) package rice noodles	$3.69
3	tbsp. soy sauce	$0.27
1	tbsp. fish sauce	$0.20
1	tbsp. chili sauce	$0.07
1	tbsp. brown sugar	$0.02
1	tbsp. lime juice	$0.09
½	cup chicken broth	$0.20
2	tbsp. canola oil	$0.06
2	eggs, beaten	$0.11
1	grated carrot	$0.16
1	tbsp. chopped garlic	$0.05
2	cups bean sprouts	$1.33
4	thinly sliced scallions (reserve 1 scallion for Round 2 Recipe, page 237)	$0.52
¼	cup coarsely chopped peanuts	$0.23
¼	cup roughly chopped fresh cilantro	$0.08

Bring a large pot of water to a boil and turn off the heat. Add the rice noodles to soften, about 20 minutes. Drain. (Reserve ½ cup cooked noodles for Round 2 Recipe: Summer Rolls, page 238.)

For the sauce: In a small bowl, whisk together the soy sauce, fish sauce, chili sauce, brown sugar, lime juice, and broth. Set aside.

In a wok or a large skillet over high heat, add 1 tablespoon oil. When it is hot, add the eggs and cook until they are firm. Remove them from the pan and let them cool a bit. Roughly chop them and set aside.

Add the remaining oil to the pan along with the carrots. Cook 1 minute, then add the garlic. Add the bean sprouts and scallions. Stir-fry 1 minute. Add the noodles and toss to combine. Add the reserved sauce and eggs, stirring to coat everything completely. Cook for another minute. Serve garnished with peanuts and cilantro.

Perfect Pad Thai for over 80% less than you would pay for takeout!

SERVES: 4
COOK TIME: 20 minutes
$7.08/$1.77 per person

Please see Round 2 Recipes on pages 237 and 238

RICE PUDDING WITH COCONUT MILK

	Reserved 2 cups cooked rice (page 232)	**$0.00**
2	(14-ounce) cans coconut milk	**$2.58**
⅓	cup packed brown sugar	**$0.12**
	Rind from 1 lime	**$0.33**
1	tsp. vanilla	**$0.44**
1	mango, diced	**$0.99**
¼	cup sweetened shredded coconut	**$0.09**

In a medium pot, stir together the rice, 1½ cans of coconut milk (reserve ½ can coconut milk for Round 2 Recipe: Coconut Chicken Soup, page 237), sugar, and lime peel. Put the pot over medium heat, bring it to a simmer, and cover. Cook until the pudding becomes very thick, about 20–25 minutes.

While the pudding is cooking, toast the shredded coconut in a dry skillet over medium heat until golden brown.

Remove the lime peel from the pudding and stir in the vanilla. Serve the rice pudding topped with diced mango and sprinkled with toasted coconut.

SERVES: 4
COOK TIME: 25 minutes
$4.55/$1.14 per person

Please see Round 2 Recipe on page 237

THAI ICED TEA

4	tea bags, black or orange pekoe	$0.12
1	(12-ounce) can sweetened condensed milk	$1.32
1	orange, sliced for garnish	$0.50
4	ounces orange vodka, optional	$2.12

In a large pot over high heat, bring 6 cups of water to a boil. Remove from the heat and add the tea bags. Steep for 10 minutes, remove the tea bags, and let cool. Pour into a clean container and chill.

Fill four tall glasses with ice. Pour the tea three-quarters of the way up and top each with sweetened condensed milk. Serve garnished with an orange slice. For the adults, top with vodka.

SERVES: 4
COOK TIME: 5 minutes
$1.94/$0.49 per person

COCONUT CHICKEN SOUP

	Reserved chicken legs, thighs, wings, and bones (page 232)	$0.00
	Reserved coconut milk (page 235)	$0.00
¼	tsp. cayenne pepper	$0.03
	1-inch piece ginger root, cut into matchsticks	$0.25
	Reserved thinly sliced scallion (page 234)	$0.00
2	tbsp. fresh lime juice	$0.22
2	tbsp. chopped fresh cilantro	$0.02
	Kosher salt, to taste	$0.00
	Black pepper, to taste	$0.00

Put the chicken into a large pot, cover it with water, and add a big pinch of salt. Cover, and bring to a boil over high heat. Reduce to a simmer, skim the scum, and cook until the chicken is cooked through, about 35–40 minutes. Remove the chicken. When cool enough to handle, shred the meat and discard the skin and bones. Strain the broth and put it back into the pot over medium heat. Add the coconut milk, cayenne pepper, and ginger, and simmer for 10 minutes. Add the chicken, scallion, and lime juice. Taste, and adjust the seasoning with salt and pepper. Serve in bowls garnished with cilantro.

TIP: Heavy cream is common in rice pudding, but coconut milk will add great flavor and save money, too!

SERVES: 4
COOK TIME: 30 minutes
$0.52 in extra ingredients

Please see Main Recipes on pages 232, 234, and 235

SUMMER ROLLS

PEANUT DIPPING SAUCE:

¼	cup chunky peanut butter	$0.17
3	tbsp. warm water	$0.00
1	tsp. soy sauce	$0.03
½	tsp. chopped garlic	$0.01
¼	tsp. red pepper flakes	$0.02
8	round rice-paper wrappers	$0.69
	Reserved rice noodles	$0.00
	(page 234)	
1	small cucumber, seeds	$0.75
	removed, cut into matchsticks	
1	carrot, cut into matchsticks	$0.16
1	mint sprig, leaves only	$0.02

In a bowl, whisk together the peanut butter, water, soy sauce, garlic, and red pepper flakes, and set aside.

Fill a shallow baking dish or pie plate with hot water. Soak a rice-paper wrapper until softened, about 30 seconds. Place it on your work surface. Along the bottom edge, layer ⅛ of the noodles, cucumber, carrot, and mint leaves. Fold up the bottom edge over the filling. Fold in the sides and continue rolling up from the bottom. Repeat with remaining rice-paper wrappers.

Serve with the dipping sauce.

SERVES: 4

$1.85 in extra ingredients

Please see Main Recipe on page 234

22. COMFORTING SOUL FOOD

- Soul-food standards at bargain-basement prices.
- **Meal #1 total: $14.79/$3.70 per person**
  Fried Chicken with Collard Greens, Sweet Tea
  Cocktail, and Banana Pudding
- **Meal #2 total: $13.61/$3.40 per person**
  Fried Pork Chops with Butter Beans, Sweet Tea
  Cocktail, and Banana Pudding

1. Light and Crispy Fried Chicken with Collard Greens

Total cost: $11.02/$2.75 per person

2. Fried Pork Chops with Buttered Beans

Total cost: $10.30/$2.58 per person

3. Sweet Tea Cocktail

Total cost: $0.32/$0.04 per person

Add an ounce of lemon vodka for just $0.52 more per cocktail

4. Banana Pudding

Total cost: $3.45/$0.86 per person

5. R2R: Bean Dip

$1.28 in extra ingredients

6. R2R: Pork Parmesan

$3.10 in extra ingredients

MSM TIP:

Loin chops have less fat than other
cuts, giving you more for your money
Pork chops, loin center cut = $2.69/lb
Pork chops, loin end cut = $1.49/lb
Savings = $1.20/lb or 45%

LIGHT AND CRISPY FRIED CHICKEN WITH COLLARD GREENS

1	whole chicken (3½- to 4-pound), cut into parts	$5.92
2	cups buttermilk	$0.32
1	tbsp. hot sauce	$0.06
1	cup flour	$0.14
1	tsp. baking soda	$0.02
½	tsp. cayenne pepper	$0.06
1	tsp. poultry seasoning	$0.03
4	cups canola oil	$1.92
	Kosher salt, to taste	$0.00
	Black pepper, to taste	$0.00

In a large bowl, mix together buttermilk, hot sauce, salt, and pepper. Add chicken parts and turn to coat completely. Marinate in refrigerator for 30 minutes–2 hours.

In a deep heavy-bottomed skillet, heat canola oil over medium-high heat. Place flour in a shallow baking dish or pie plate, stir in baking soda, cayenne pepper, poultry seasoning, salt, and pepper. Place chicken pieces in flour mixture, shake off excess. Fry in hot oil until golden brown on outside and cooked through, about 12–15 minutes. Frying chicken in batches will avoid overcrowding in skillet. Remove from oil and drain on a paper-lined sheet tray.

SERVES: 4
COOK TIME: 12–15 minutes
$8.47/$2.11 per person

COLLARD GREENS

2	bunches collard greens	$1.58
3	strips bacon	$0.51
1	medium sliced yellow onion	$0.28
1	tbsp. garlic	$0.07
½	tsp. red pepper flakes	$0.04
1	tbsp. brown sugar	$0.02
2	tbsp. cider vinegar	$0.05
	Kosher salt, to taste	$0.00
	Black pepper, to taste	$0.00

In a high-sided skillet, cook bacon. Remove, and drain on paper towels. In the same pan, sauté the onions until translucent, about 5 minutes. Add the garlic, red pepper flakes, brown sugar, cider vinegar, and salt and pepper, to taste. Cook for 1 minute more.

Strip leaves from the tough stems of the collard greens and chop into 2-inch pieces. Add greens, sugar, salt, and pepper to the pan, and stir. Cover and cook for 10–15 minutes, stirring halfway through. Collards are done when tender and lack bitterness. Remove from heat. Roughly chop bacon and stir into greens.

SERVES: 4
COOK TIME: 15 minutes
$2.55/$0.64 per person

FRIED PORK CHOPS WITH BUTTERED BEANS

6	pork chops, loin end cut (about 3 pounds)	$4.77
1	cup canola oil	$0.48
½	cup flour	$0.10
¼	cup bread crumbs	$0.14
¼	cup cornmeal	$0.06
1½	tsp. Italian seasoning	$0.09
1	tsp. paprika	$0.08
1	tsp. garlic powder	$0.06
	Kosher salt, to taste	$0.00
	Black pepper, to taste	$0.00

FOR BUTTERED BEANS:

4	tbsp. butter	$0.25
1	medium chopped yellow onion	$0.28
1	thick (2-ounce) slice deli ham, chopped	$0.75
1	(10-ounce) box frozen lima beans, thawed	$3.00
	Kosher salt, to taste	$0.00
	Black pepper, to taste	$0.00

In a heavy-bottomed skillet, heat canola oil over medium-high heat.

Season pork chops on all sides generously with salt and pepper. In a shallow baking dish or pie plate, combine the flour with cornmeal, bread crumbs, Italian seasoning, garlic powder, paprika, and salt and pepper, to taste. Place each chop in flour mixture, coating completely and shaking off excess. Fry in hot oil until golden brown on both sides and cooked through, about 3–4 minutes each side. Remove from oil and drain on a sheet pan lined with a brown paper bag. (Reserve 2 chops for Round 2 Recipe: Pork Parmesan, page 248.)

FOR BUTTERED BEANS:

In a large skillet, melt 1 tablespoon butter, add diced ham, and sauté until lightly browned. Remove ham from pan and reserve on a plate. Add remaining butter, onions, salt, and pepper. Sauté until translucent. Add lima beans and continue cooking for 5 minutes. (Reserve 2 cups sautéed beans and onions for Round 2 Recipe: Bean Dip, page 247.) Return cooked ham to pan, stir to combine, and serve along with fried pork chops.

SERVES: 4
COOK TIME: 18 minutes
$10.06/$2.51 per person

Please see Round 2 Recipes on pages 247 and 248

SWEET TEA COCKTAIL

8	cups brewed black tea (use 6 tea bags)	$0.18
½	cup sugar	$0.10
2	sprigs mint	$0.04
6	ounces lemon-flavored vodka, optional	$3.18

In a small saucepan over medium heat, combine sugar with ½ cup of water. Add mint. Bring to a boil, stirring to dissolve the sugar, and remove from heat to cool.

In a large pitcher, stir together the tea and simple syrup. Add vodka, if using. Serve chilled over ice with a lemon-wedge garnish.

SERVES: 8
COOK TIME: 5 minutes
$0.32/$0.04 per person

BANANA PUDDING

1	box instant vanilla pudding	$0.33
2	cups milk	$0.32
2	bananas, sliced	$0.60
2	cups (about ⅓ box) vanilla wafers	$0.66

FOR WHIPPED CREAM TOPPING:

1	cup heavy cream, very cold	$1.12
3	tbsp. confectioners' sugar	$0.04
1	tsp. pumpkin pie spice (for garnish)	$0.38

Prepare pudding according to package directions.

In each serving glass, put down a layer of vanilla wafers, and top it with about 3 tablespoons of pudding mix, then a few slices of banana. Continue in this way, creating three layers and finishing with a pudding layer. Allow to sit in refrigerator for at least 1 hour, and up to overnight, to set and soften cookies.

In a clean bowl, beat together cream with confectioners' sugar until soft peaks form.

Top each dessert with a generous dollop of whipped cream. Garnish with pumpkin pie spice and a vanilla wafer.

SERVES: 4
$3.45/$0.86 per person

BEAN DIP

	Reserved beans and onions (page 244)	$0.00
2	tsp. minced garlic	$0.05
2	tbsp. Parmesan cheese	$0.54
2	tbsp. chopped fresh basil	$0.04
2	tbsp. lemon juice	$0.15
¼	tsp. red pepper flakes	$0.02
¼	cup olive oil	$0.48
	Kosher salt, to taste	$0.00
	Black pepper, to taste	$0.00

In a food processor, pulse half of the beans, ¼ cup of water, and all other ingredients except the olive oil, until smooth. Slowly pour in olive oil with machine running. When incorporated, add the remainder of beans and onions, and pulse until just combined but still chunky.

SERVES: 4

$1.28 in extra ingredients

Please see Main Recipe on page 244

PORK PARMESAN

1	tbsp. olive oil	$0.12
2	tsp. minced garlic	$0.05
½	tsp. Italian seasoning	$0.03
1	(15-ounce) can tomato sauce	$1.19
1	tbsp. chopped fresh basil	$0.02
	Reserved pork chops (page 244)	$0.00
2	tbsp. Parmesan cheese	$0.27
½	cup grated mozzarella	$0.44
2	hoagie rolls, toasted	$1.13
¼	tsp. kosher salt	$0.00
¼	tsp. black pepper	$0.00

In a small saucepan, heat 1 tablespoon olive oil. Add garlic, Italian seasoning, salt, and pepper, and cook 1 minute. Add tomato sauce and bring to a simmer. Take off heat. Stir in basil.

Preheat oven to 425°F.

Remove pork chops from bone and slice into large strips. Place sliced pork chop on roll. Cover each with the tomato sauce, sprinkle with Parmesan cheese, and top with mozzarella cheese.

Place in oven and bake for 10 minutes or until cheese is bubbling and chop is heated through.

TIP: *Toasting the bread before topping with the pork, sauce, and cheese will help prevent soggy sandwiches.*

SERVES: 2
COOK TIME: 10 minutes
$3.10 in extra ingredients

Please see Main Recipe on page 244

23. THRIFTY TEX MEX

- Money Saving Meals is heading to the Lone-Star State for some authentic Tex-Mex flavors that won't scorch your budget.
- Spicy southwestern flavors at a price that won't make you sweat.
- **Meal #1 total: $10.11/$2.52 per person**
  Grilled Tex-Mex Pork Chops, a Mango Margarita, and Spicy Corn Bread
- **Meal #2 total: $15.41/$3.85 per person**
  Beanless Beef Chili, a Mango Margarita, and Spicy Corn Bread

---

1. Grilled Tex-Mex Pork Chops
Total cost: $5.27/$1.32 per serving

Start by making your own seasoning rub. That way you can control what is in it, and just look at the savings . . .

> **MSM TIP:**
> Packet Tex-Mex seasoning = $0.99
> Sandra's Tex-Mex seasoning = $0.17
> Savings = $0.82 or 83%

2. Beanless Beef Chili
Total cost: $10.57/$2.52 per person

3. Mango Margarita
Total cost: $2.95/$0.74 per person

4. Spicy Corn Bread
Total cost: $1.89/$0.47 per person

> **MSM TIP:**
> Fresh-baked bread at the grocery store = $3.49
> Sandra's corn bread = $1.89
> Savings = $1.60 or 46%

5. R2R: Beef and Bean Burritos
$3.11 in extra ingredients

6. R2R: Pork Corn Bread Bites
$0.36 in extra ingredients

GRILLED TEX-MEX PORK CHOPS

3	tbsp. canola oil	$0.06
1	tbsp. chopped garlic	$0.05
1	tbsp. chili powder,	$0.06
	divided use	
1	tbsp. oregano	$0.02
½	tsp. red pepper flakes	$0.04
1½	pounds bone-in pork chops,	$2.24
	about 5	
1	(15-ounce) can	$0.99
	chopped tomatoes	
1	head shredded green cabbage	$1.74
2	tbsp. apple cider vinegar	$0.06
2	tsp. brown sugar	$0.01
	Kosher salt, to taste	$0.00

In a large resealable plastic bag, mix together 2 tablespoons oil, garlic, 2 teaspoons chili powder, oregano, and red pepper flakes. Add the pork chops, seal, and mix everything together. Put the bag into a bowl and refrigerate for at least 2 hours or up to overnight. Heat your outdoor grill or a grill pan.

Remove the chops from the marinade, cover, and bring them to room temperature. Pour the marinade into a saucepan, add half the tomatoes (reserve the rest for the Round 2 Recipe: Beef and Bean Burritos, page 258), bring to a boil, and cook until slightly thickened, about 5 minutes. Remove half the sauce to put on cooked chops.

Grill the chops quickly on high heat, about 2 minutes per side. Move them to a cooler part of the grill. Brush some sauce on both sides and cook on low for 1 minute. Keep brushing and turning the chops, until they are nicely glazed and cooked through, about 10 minutes. Serve with the cabbage and the reserved sauce on the side. (Reserve 1 pork chop for the Round 2 Recipe: Pork Corn Bread Bites, page 260.)

While the chops are cooking, make the cabbage. Shred half the head. (Reserve remaining half for Round 2 Recipe, page 258.) In a large skillet over medium-high heat, add the remaining 1 tablespoon oil. When it is hot, add the cabbage along with the vinegar, remaining chili powder, sugar, and salt to taste. Stir it well and cook until the cabbage is wilted and just tender, about 5–6 minutes.

Please see Round 2 Recipes on pages 258 and 260

SERVES: 4
COOK TIME: 30 minutes
$5.27/$1.32 per person

BEANLESS BEEF CHILI

2	tbsp. canola oil	$0.06
1	(2½-pound) beef chuck roast, cut into ½-inch cubes	$8.73
2	medium chopped yellow onions	$0.56
1	tbsp. chili powder	$0.06
½	tsp. red pepper flakes	$0.04
½	tsp. cinnamon	$0.05
1	small chopped jalapeño pepper	$0.29
1	tbsp. chopped garlic	$0.05
1	(28-ounce) can chopped tomatoes	$0.99
1	cup beef broth	$0.40
	Kosher salt, to taste	$0.00
	Black pepper, to taste	$0.00

SPICED SOUR CREAM

½	cup sour cream	$0.19
1	tsp. chili powder	$0.02
1	tsp. lime juice	$0.11
1	tsp. hot sauce	$0.02
2	scallions	$0.26
2	tbsp. chopped fresh cilantro	$0.02

Put a deep heavy-bottomed pot over medium-high heat and add the oil. Put in the beef, season with salt and pepper, and cook until it is well browned, about 10–15 minutes. Remove the meat to a bowl with a slotted spoon and discard the fat from the pan. Pour half the broth into the pan and scrape up any browned bits.

Pour this into the bowl of a slow cooker. Add the onions and put the meat on top. Add the chili seasoning, red pepper flakes, cinnamon, jalapeño, and garlic.

Add the tomatoes with their juice and the remaining broth. Cover and cook on low for 4–6 hours. Taste, and adjust the seasoning. (Reserve 1 cup for the Round 2 Recipe: Beef and Bean Burritos, page 258.) Serve garnished with spiced sour cream.

SERVES: 4
COOK TIME: 2 hours
$10.57/$2.52 per person

Please see Round 2 Recipe on page 258

MANGO MARGARITA

1	(1-liter) container	
	mango nectar	**$1.79**
	Juice of 1 orange	**$0.50**
2	limes	**$0.66**
	Tequila, optional	**$1.52/4oz**
	Kosher salt	**$0.00**

Dip the rims of four highball glasses in water, then dip them in salt spread out on a plate. Fill them with ice and set aside.

Into a blender, pour the mango nectar, orange juice, and juice of 1 lime. Blend until smooth. Pour into the prepared glasses and garnish with lime wedges. Add tequila, if using.

SERVES: 4
$2.95/$0.74 per person

SPICY CORN BREAD

2	tbsp. canola oil	**$0.06**
1	medium chopped yellow onion	**$0.28**
2	cups cornmeal	**$0.24**
1	cup baking mix	**$0.30**
½	cup sugar	**$0.10**
2	tsp. baking soda	**$0.02**
1	tsp. salt	**$0.00**
½	tsp. cayenne pepper	**$0.06**
2	cups milk	**$0.32**
2	large eggs	**$0.22**
1	jalapeño, finely chopped	**$0.29**

Heat the oven to 375°F.

Put a 10-inch cast-iron skillet over medium-high heat, and add the oil. When the oil is hot, add the onions and cook until soft and beginning to brown, about 8–10 minutes. Remove onions from the pan and spoon onto brown paper to drain. Leave remaining oil in the pan.

In a large bowl, whisk together the cornmeal, baking mix, sugar, baking soda, salt, and cayenne. In another bowl, whisk together the milk and eggs. Add the wet ingredients to the dry ingredients, and stir until combined. Fold in reserved onions and jalapeño pepper. Pour the batter into the skillet and bake about 20–25 minutes. (Reserve 2 pieces corn bread for Round 2 Recipe, page 260.)

SERVES: 4
COOK TIME: 35 minutes
$1.89/$0.47 per person

Please see Round 2 Recipe on page 260

BEEF AND BEAN BURRITOS

4	large flour tortillas	$0.72
	Reserved tomato (page 252)	$0.00
	Reserved chopped cabbage (page 252)	$0.00
1	medium chopped red onion	$0.67
1	tbsp. chopped fresh cilantro	$0.02
1	tbsp. canola oil	$0.03
	Reserved chili (page 254)	$0.00
1	(15-ounce) can black beans, rinsed and drained	$0.67
1	cup shredded Monterey Jack cheese	$1.00

Heat the oven to 350°F. Wrap the tortillas in a damp towel and microwave them for 30 seconds to make them warm and pliable.

In a bowl, mix together the reserved tomatoes, cabbage, half the onion, and the cilantro. Set the salsa aside.

In a small pot over medium-high heat, add the oil. When it is hot, add the remaining onion and cook until soft, about 6–8 minutes. Add the reserved chili and the beans. Stir and cook until hot.

Place a tortilla on your work surface and spread ¼ of the chili-and-bean mixture down the middle. Sprinkle with 2 tablespoons of cheese and roll up like a cigar, tucking in the ends. Place it onto a baking dish and make three more. Sprinkle the remaining cheese over the top and bake in the oven until the cheese is melted and browned, about 10 minutes. Serve topped with the cabbage salsa.

SERVES: 4

COOK TIME: 20 minutes

$3.11 in extra ingredients

Please see Main Recipes on pages 252 and 254

PORK CORN BREAD BITES

2	tbsp. unsalted butter	$0.12
	Reserved corn bread, sliced through the middle (page 256)	$0.00
	Reserved pork chop (page 252)	$0.00
2	tbsp. brown sugar	$0.04
1	tbsp. soy sauce	$0.09
2	tsp. hot sauce	$0.04
2	tbsp. sour cream	$0.05
1	tbsp. chopped fresh cilantro	$0.02

In a nonstick skillet over medium heat, melt the butter. When it is bubbling, add the corn bread, and cook until it is browned on each side, about 5 minutes total. Remove from the pan and set aside.

Add the pork chop to the pan and cook until it is warmed through, about 5 minutes. Remove and set aside.

To the pan, add the sugar, soy sauce, and hot sauce, and cook until the sugar is melted and the sauce thickens slightly, about 5 minutes.

To assemble, cut the corn bread and pork chop into 1-inch pieces. Place a piece of corn bread on a plate, top it with a piece of pork, and drizzle it with the sauce. Top with another piece of corn bread and secure with a toothpick. Place a small dollop of sour cream on each bite and sprinkle with the cilantro.

SERVES: 4
COOK TIME: 10 minutes
$0.36 in extra ingredients

Please see Main Recipes on pages 252 and 256

Try serving these bites with fresh mixed greens

24. FLASH IN THE PAN

- Perfect picnic recipes—if you follow my lead you will save yourself enough money to put a really nice bottle of wine in that picnic basket.
- **Meal #1 total: $18.27/$4.56 per person**
  - Chicken Cutlet Sandwich with Herb Mayo, Corn Salad, Blueberry Scones with Lemon Glaze, and Raspberry Lemonade
- **Meal #2 total: $16.18/$4.05 per person**
  - Garlicky Hummus and Cucumber Sandwich, Blueberry Scones with Lemon Glaze, and Raspberry Lemonade

---

1. Chicken Cutlet Sandwich with Herb Mayonnaise
Total cost: $8.83/$2.21 per person

2. Garlicky Hummus and Cucumber Sandwich
Total cost: $6.74/$1.69 per person

3. Corn Salad
Total cost: $3.28/$0.82 per person

4. Blueberry Scones with Lemon Glaze
Total cost: $3.01/$0.75 per person

In this recipe we are saving 50% over the same amount of store-bought mix you would need

> **MSM TIP:**
> Fresh = $2.50
> Frozen = $1.00
> Savings = $1.50 or 60%

5. Raspberry Lemonade
Total cost: $3.15/$0.79 per person

6. R2R: Corn Puddings
$0.97 in extra ingredients

7. R2R: Tomato, Cucumber, and White Bean Salad
$1.25 in extra ingredients

CHICKEN CUTLET SANDWICH WITH HERB MAYONNAISE

1½	pounds bone-in	$4.49
	chicken breast	
	Canola oil, for brushing	$0.06
½	cup mayonnaise	$0.52
1	tbsp. spicy brown mustard	$0.04
	Zest of 1 lemon (reserve	$0.00
	the juice for Blueberry Scones,	
	page 268)	
2	tbsp. chopped fresh parsley	$0.02
2	tbsp. fennel fronds	$0.12
1	baguette, about 16 inches long	$1.99
½	medium red onion, sliced thin	$0.34
½	small shredded head lettuce	$1.25
	Kosher salt, to taste	$0.00
	Black pepper, to taste	$0.00

Heat your grill or a grill pan over medium-high heat.

Remove the skin from the chicken and take the meat off the bone. Slice the breast horizontally across to make four thin pieces. Pound the chicken lightly between 2 pieces of plastic wrap. Season the cutlets with salt and pepper and brush them with a little oil. Grill the cutlets until cooked through, about 5 minutes per side. Let cool.

Put the mayonnaise into a bowl with the mustard, lemon zest, parsley, and fennel fronds. Whisk to combine. Check the seasoning and add salt and pepper to taste. Cut the baguette in half lengthwise. Spread the herb mayonnaise on the bottom half. Top with the chicken, onions, and lettuce. Spread the remaining mayonnaise on the other half of the baguette, and place it on top. Cut the sandwich into 4 pieces and wrap well in wax paper or plastic wrap.

SERVES: 4
COOK TIME: 10 minutes
$8.83/$2.21 per person

GARLICKY HUMMUS AND CUCUMBER SANDWICH

1	head garlic	$0.70
¼	cup extra-virgin olive oil	$0.96
2	(15-ounce) cans white beans	$1.34
8	slices whole wheat bread	$1.25
2	large cucumbers	$1.32
3	Roma tomatoes	$1.17
	Kosher salt, to taste	$0.00
	Black pepper, to taste	$0.00

Heat the oven to 375°F.

Cut the top off the garlic head, drizzle with 1 teaspoon of olive oil, wrap in aluminum foil, and bake until soft, about 45 minutes–1 hour. Unwrap and allow to cool.

Drain and rinse the beans. (Reserve ½ cup beans for the Round 2 Recipe: Tomato, Cucumber, and White Bean Salad, page 273.) Put them in a food processor with ¼ cup olive oil. Squeeze in the roasted garlic and season with salt and pepper. Process until smooth and about the consistency of mayonnaise, adding some water if it is too thick. (Reserve 2 tablespoons of the hummus for Round 2 Recipe: Tomato, Cucumber, and White Bean Salad, page 273.)

Spread the hummus on each slice of bread. Top four pieces with cucumber and tomato slices and put the remaining pieces of bread on top to make a sandwich. (Reserve ½ of the cucumber and ½ tomato for the Round 2 Recipe, page 273.) Cut the sandwiches in half and wrap them well with wax paper or plastic wrap.

SERVES: 4
COOK TIME: 45-60 minutes
$6.74/$1.69 per person

Please see Round 2 Recipe on page 273

CORN SALAD

2	cups frozen corn, thawed	$1.00
1	Granny Smith apple, peeled and chopped	$0.48
1	fennel bulb	$0.99
½	medium chopped red onion	$0.34
2	tbsp. chopped fresh parsley	$0.02
1	tsp. ground cumin	$0.11
2	tbsp. apple cider vinegar	$0.06
1	tbsp. spicy brown mustard	$0.04
¼	cup canola oil	$0.24
	Kosher salt, to taste	$0.00
	Black pepper, to taste	$0.00

In a bowl, toss together the corn, apple, fennel, and onion. (Reserve 1 cup mixture for Round 2 Recipe: Corn Puddings, page 272.) Add the parsley and cumin and season with salt and pepper. In a small bowl, whisk together the vinegar, mustard, and oil. (Reserve 2 tablespoons of the vinaigrette for Round 2 Recipe: Tomato, Cucumber, and White Bean Salad, page 273.) Add the dressing to the vegetables and toss well to coat.

SERVES: 4
$3.28/$0.82 per person

Please see Round 2 Recipes on pages 272 and 273

BLUEBERRY SCONES WITH LEMON GLAZE

2½	cups Bisquick baking mix	$0.75
¼	cup sugar	$0.05
½	stick (¼ cup) unsalted butter	$0.24
2	large eggs	$0.22
¼	cup milk	$0.04
½	cup frozen blueberries	$0.73
	Flour for dusting	$0.03
1	cup confectioners' sugar	$0.23
	Reserved juice of 1 lemon	$0.50
½	tsp. vanilla	$0.22

Heat the oven to 400°F.

For the scones: Whisk together the baking mix and sugar. Mix in the butter with your hands or a pastry blender until the butter is the size of peas. Beat the eggs well with ¼ cup of milk. Pour the wet ingredients into the dry ingredients and mix just until blended. Avoid overmixing. Gently fold in the blueberries. Turn the dough out onto a floured surface and pat into a ¾-inch-thick square. Cut into four squares and cut each square into two triangles. Place the scones onto an ungreased baking sheet and bake until golden brown, about 15 minutes or so. Remove to a wire rack and cool a bit before glazing.

For the glaze: Whisk together the confectioners' sugar, lemon juice, and vanilla until smooth. Pour evenly over the still-warm scones.

SERVES: 4
COOK TIME: 15 minutes
$3.01/$0.75 per person

RASPBERRY LEMONADE

½	cup frozen raspberries	$1.00
¾	cup sugar	$0.15
4	lemons	$2.00
4	ounces raspberry or citrus vodka, optional	$2.12
1	quart cold water	$0.00

Reserve 4 raspberries and 4 slices of lemon for garnish. Mash the raspberries and sugar together and let sit at room temperature to thaw and bring out their juices. Set a sieve over a pitcher and juice the lemons. Rinse the sieve. Push the raspberry mixture through the sieve with a rubber spatula, leaving the seeds in the sieve. Pour 1 quart of cold water through the sieve to get out the remaining juices. Stir the lemonade and check for sweetness. Serve over ice, garnished with a lemon slice and raspberry. For the adults, add 1 ounce vodka to each glass.

SERVES: 4
$3.15/$0.79 per person

CORN PUDDINGS

1	tbsp. butter	$0.06
	Reserved Corn Salad	$0.00
	(page 266)	
2	large eggs	$0.22
½	cup milk	$0.08
½	tsp. vanilla	$0.22
1	tsp. sugar	$0.01
¼	cup grated Cheddar cheese	$0.38
	Kosher salt, to taste	$0.00

Heat the oven to 350°F.

Put a kettle of water on to boil. Butter 4 (8-ounce) ramekins. Have a baking pan large enough to fit the ramekins ready.

Divide the Corn Salad evenly among the ramekins. In a bowl, whisk together the eggs, milk, sugar, vanilla, and salt to taste. Pour the egg mixture evenly among the ramekins. Top each with a tablespoon of cheese.

Place the ramekins in the baking pan and put the pan in the oven. Pour enough hot water to come halfway up the ramekins. Bake until set, about 30–35 minutes.

SERVES: 4

COOK TIME: 35 minutes

$0.97 in extra ingredients

Please see Main Recipe on page 266

TOMATO, CUCUMBER, AND WHITE BEAN SALAD

½	reserved tomato, chopped	$0.00
¼	reserved English cucumber, chopped	$0.00
½	cup reserved white beans	$0.00
	Reserved hummus (page 265)	$0.00
	Reserved vinaigrette (page 266)	$0.00
½	small head lettuce, shredded	$1.25
	Kosher salt, to taste	$0.00
	Black pepper, to taste	$0.00

Put the tomatoes, cucumber, and white beans into a bowl and toss to combine. Whisk together the hummus and vinaigrette. Toss with the bean mixture. Taste, and adjust seasoning with the salt and pepper. Spread the lettuce onto a platter and top with the bean mixture.

SERVES: 4

$1.25 in extra ingredients

Please see Main Recipes on pages 265 and 266

25. SMART, SIMPLE SERVING

- A fabulous tea party at a price that won't get you steamed!
- Meal # 1 total: $13.97/$3.50 per person

    Ham and Egg Tea Sandwiches, Crispy Wonton Cups with

    Tuna Salad, Crunchy Coated Chocolate Truffles, and

    a Chamomile Cooler

1. Ham and Egg Tea Sandwiches

Total cost: $4.67/$1.17 per person

2. Crispy Wonton Cups with Tuna Salad

Total cost: $5.22/$0.44 per person

3. Crunchy Coated Chocolate Truffles

Total cost: $2.96/$0.15 per person

4. Chamomile Cooler

Total cost: $1.12/$0.28 per cocktail

> To turn this mocktail into a cocktail, add 4 ounces of
> white wine for another $2.12 per cocktail. Cheers!

5. R2R: Niçoise Salad with Lemon Garlic Vinaigrette

$2.85 in extra ingredients

6. R2R: Ham and Cheese Breakfast Burritos

$1.28 in extra ingredients

MSM TIP:

Prepackaged ham slices
= $7.98/lb
Deli sliced ham = $4.99/lb
Savings = $2.99 or 37%

MSM TIP:

Store-bought milk chocolate
truffles = $5.82
SL's truffles = $3.25
Savings = $2.57 or 44%

MSM TIP:

Frozen store-bought phyllo
cups = $1.80
SL's wonton cups = $0.75
Savings = $1.05 or 58%

HAM AND EGG TEA SANDWICHES

HAM SALAD

½	pound deli ham, sliced thick and diced (reserve 4 slices for Round 2 Recipe, page 282)	$2.50
1	tbsp. pickle relish	$0.05
2	tbsp. mayonnaise	$0.06
1	tbsp. spicy brown mustard	$0.04
1	tbsp. chopped fresh parsley	$0.02
1	tbsp. finely diced yellow onion	$0.01
1	stalk celery	$0.15
	Kosher salt, to taste	$0.00
	Black pepper, to taste	$0.00

EGG SALAD

6	large eggs, hard boiled, diced (reserve 2 eggs for Round 2 Recipe, page 280)	$0.66
2	tbsp. mayonnaise	$0.06
1	tbsp. chopped fresh dill	$0.02
¼	tsp. paprika	$0.02
6	slices whole wheat bread, crust removed	$0.60
6	slices white bread, crust removed	$0.48

In a medium bowl, whisk together mayonnaise and mustard. Add ham, pickle relish, parsley, onion, and celery, and toss to coat. Set aside.

In another bowl, gently toss together the chopped eggs, mayonnaise, dill, and paprika.

Alternating between white and whole wheat bread, place 4 slices of bread down, spread ¼ of ham salad on top of each slice, top with the other type of bread, spread ¼ of egg salad mixture on each slice, and finally top with same type of bread as the bottom. Cut off the crusts and slice the bread crosswise into 4 triangles.

SERVES: 4
$4.67/$1.17 PER PERSON

Please see Round 2 Recipes on pages 280 and 282

CRISPY WONTON CUPS WITH TUNA SALAD

12	square wonton wrappers	$0.75
	Cooking spray	$0.00
1	(12-ounce) can chunk light tuna (reserve ½ can for Round 2 Recipe, page 280)	$1.99
2	tsp. spicy brown mustard	$0.02
1	tbsp. canola oil	$0.03
2	tsp. red wine vinegar	$0.02
½	tsp. minced ginger	$0.04
1	medium chopped red onion (reserve all but 1 tbsp. for Round 2 Recipe, page 282)	$0.68
1½	cups snow peas (reserve 1¼ cups for Round 2 Recipe, page 280)	$1.62
⅛	tsp. red pepper flakes	$0.01
3	tbsp. chopped fresh parsley (reserve 2 tbsp. for Round 2 Recipe, page 280)	$0.06
	Kosher salt, to taste	$0.00
	Black pepper, to taste	$0.00

Preheat oven to 375°F. Coat the muffin tin with the cooking spray.

Place one wonton wrapper into each cup. Press the wontons into the cups with your fingers, and spray each wrapper with cooking spray. Bake until golden brown, about 5–6 minutes. Remove from the oven and let cool.

In a bowl, whisk together the oil, mustard, vinegar, and ginger. Stir in tuna, onion, snow peas, and red pepper flakes, and season with salt and pepper.

Spoon about a tablespoon of the tuna salad into each wonton cup, garnish with fresh parsley, and serve.

SERVES: 12
COOK TIME: 3 minutes
$5.22/$0.44 per person

Please see Round 2 Recipes on pages 280 and 282

CRUNCHY COATED CHOCOLATE TRUFFLES

1	(12-ounce) bag chocolate chips	$2.39
⅔	cup light cream	$0.58
½	tsp. cinnamon	$0.05
2	graham cracker boards	$0.04
½	cup coconut shreds, toasted	$0.19

In a small saucepan, heat light cream until gently boiling. Put the chocolate chips into a bowl and pour the hot cream over them. Stir until the chocolate is completely melted. Separate chocolate ("ganache") into two small bowls and stir the cinnamon into one bowl.

Put the ganache into the refrigerator until it firms up, about 1½–2 hours. In the meantime, place graham cracker boards in a food-storage bag and crush with your hands to make crumbs. Put the crumbs and the toasted coconut on separate flat plates.

Remove the ganache from the refrigerator. Using a tablespoon, scoop out the chocolate and roll it in the palms of your hands to form small balls. Work quickly to prevent the chocolate from melting. Roll the truffles in the toppings—the cinnamon-flavored in graham cracker crumbs and the plain in coconut.

SERVES: 20
COOK TIME: 3 minutes
$2.96/$0.15 per person

CHAMOMILE COOLER

4	chamomile tea bags	$0.44
¼	cup dried cranberries	$0.44
½	apple, diced	$0.24
	White wine, optional	$3.18

In a pot over medium-high heat, bring 4 cups of water and the dried cranberries to a boil. Pour into a glass pitcher with tea bags and let steep for 4–5 minutes. Remove the tea bags, let cool, and refrigerate for about one hour.

Divide the apples among four wineglasses. Pour the chilled chamomile and cranberries into each glass. Add white wine, if using.

> **SERVES:** 10
> **COOK TIME:** 5 minutes
> **$1.12/$0.28 per person**

NIÇOISE SALAD WITH LEMON GARLIC VINAIGRETTE

1	head butter lettuce, washed and torn	$1.29
	Reserved hard-boiled eggs, sliced (page 276)	$0.00
	Reserved chunk light tuna (page 277)	$0.00
2	tbsp. slivered almonds	$0.13
	Reserved snow peas, blanched (page 277)	$0.00
½	medium thinly sliced red onion (reserve 2 slices for Round 2 Recipe, page 282)	$0.34
1	tbsp. capers	$0.45

LEMON GARLIC VINAIGRETTE:

	Juice and zest of 1 lemon	$0.50
1	tsp. minced garlic	$0.02
¼	cup canola oil	$0.12
	Reserved parsley (page 277)	$0.00
	Kosher salt, to taste	$0.00
	Black pepper, to taste	$0.00

In a small bowl, whisk together the lemon juice, zest, garlic, oil, and parsley, and season with salt and pepper. Set aside.

In a large bowl, toss the lettuce, snow peas, and onion with the vinaigrette. Top with the sliced eggs, tuna, almonds, and capers. Serve immediately.

> **SERVES:** 4
> **COOK TIME:** 10 minutes
> **$2.85 in extra ingredients**

Please see Main Recipes on pages 276 and 277

HAM AND CHEESE BREAKFAST BURRITOS

1	tsp. canola oil	$0.01
	Reserved ham, diced (page 276)	$0.00
	Reserved red onion, diced (page 277 or 280)	$0.00
¼	cup diced green bell pepper	$0.22
4	eggs	$0.44
	Cooking spray	$0.00
¼	cup shredded Cheddar cheese	$0.25
2	flour tortillas	$0.36
	Kosher salt, to taste	$0.00
	Black pepper, to taste	$0.00

Heat a medium skillet over medium heat and add the canola oil. When the oil is hot, cook the ham, red onion, and bell pepper until beginning to brown, about 4–5 minutes. Remove from the pan and set aside.

In a small bowl, whisk together the eggs with 1 tablespoon water and salt and pepper, to taste.

Coat the skillet with cooking spray and put it over medium-low heat. Add the beaten eggs and gently stir with a spatula or wooden spoon. Cook eggs until cooked to your liking, about 1–2 minutes. Put the cooked ham and vegetables back into the pan and stir to combine.

Wrap the tortillas in a damp towel and microwave for 30 seconds to warm them. Put a tortilla on a plate, add half egg mixture, and top with half the cheese. Wrap the ends of the tortilla up, and fold in the sides. Repeat for second burrito and serve warm.

SERVES: 2
COOK TIME: 2 minutes
$1.28 in extra ingredients

Please see Main Recipes on pages 276 and 277

Index

A

Aioli Sauce, 78

Appetizers

Bean Dip, 247

Couscous Stuffed Tomatoes, 228

Crispy Baby Potato Bites with Sour
Cream and Bacon, 124

Crispy Wonton Cups with Tuna
Salad, 277

Cucumber Cups Stuffed with
Shrimp Cocktail, 128

Eggplant Dip, 219

Grilled Corn and Bean Salsa with
Oven-Baked Corn Chips, 92–93

Ham and Egg Tea Sandwiches, 276

Shrimp Bruschetta, 228

Summer Rolls, 238

Apple

Frosty Sparkling Apple Cider, 105

Grilled Chicken and Apple
Wraps, 196

Mini Apple Spice Glazed
Donuts, 140

Roast Bone-in Pork Loin with Apple Mustard Glaze, 166

Sparkling Cider Mimosa, 142

Arroz con Pollo, 68

Asparagus

Asparagus and Tomato Tart, 136

Cream of Asparagus Soup, 144

B

Bacon

Baked Mashed Potatoes, 154

Bow Ties and Buttons, 187

Crispy Baby Potato Bites with Sour
Cream and Bacon, 124

Potato and Shrimp Salad with Sour
Cream and Bacon Dressing, 132

Spaghetti Carbonara, 202

Baked Mashed Potatoes, 154

Bananas

Banana Daiquiri, 225

Banana Pudding, 246

French Toast with Brown-Sugar
Banana Syrup, 138

Barbecue

Chicken Sliders with Spicy BBQ
Mayo, 126

Pulled Pork Sliders with Mustard
BBQ Sauce and Pickled
Onions, 96

Basil

Basil Chicken, 232

Basil Walnut Pesto, 82

Grilled Margherita Pizza, 62

Orange Basil Bellinis, 203

Shrimp Scampi over Pesto
Couscous, 222

White Chocolate-Chip Shortcake
with Basil Strawberries, 58

Beanless Beef Chili, 254

Beans

Bean Dip, 247

Beef and Bean Burritos, 258

Black Bean and Pork Stew, 74

Bow Ties and Buttons, 187

Cajun Red Bean and Rice Soup, 42

Fried Pork Chops with Buttered
Beans, 244

Garlicky Hummus and Cucumber
Sandwich, 265

Grilled Corn and Bean Salsa with
Oven-Baked Corn Chips, 92–93

Pan-Fried Tilapia with Sautéed
Edamame, 180

Pork Nachos, 98

Tomato, Cucumber, and White
Bean Salad, 273

Beef

Beanless Beef Chili, 254

Beef and Bean Burritos, 258

Beef and Mushroom Soup, 10

Beef Kebab Pita Pockets, 186

Beef Kebabs, 182

Moussaka, 212

Slow Cooker Short Ribs, 4

Steak and Cheese Hoagies, 224

Bellinis, Orange Basil, 204

Berry Custard Pie, 84

Black Bean and Pork Stew, 74

Bloody Mary, 31

Blueberries

Berry Custard Pie, 84

Blueberry Scones with Lemon
Glaze, 268

Bow Ties and Buttons, 187

Breads

Blueberry Scones with Lemon
Glaze, 268

Bread Pudding, 146

Coffee Cake, 30

French Toast with Brown-Sugar
Banana Syrup, 138

Fried Bread Pudding Bites, 50

Golden Raisin and Walnut
Stuffing, 152

Mini Apple Spice Glazed
Donuts, 140

Savory Bread Pudding with
Ham, 32

Savory Bread Pudding with
Sausage and Mushrooms, 46

Spicy Corn Bread, 256

Brown Rice and Mushroom Salad, 191

Brown Sugar and Ginger Glazed
Ham, 14

Bruschetta, Shrimp, 228

Burgers, Portobello, 78

Burritos

Beef and Bean Burritos, 258

Ham and Cheese Breakfast
Burritos, 282

C

Cabbage

Cabbage and Pear Slaw, 108

German Dumpling Soup, 109

Grilled Tex-Mex Pork Chops, 252

Slow-Cooked Orange Pork-
Shoulder Tacos with Cabbage
Slaw, 90

Cajun Catfish Cakes with Creamy
Remoulade, 36

Cajun Quesadilla, 42

Cajun Red Bean and Rice Soup, 42

Cakes

Coffee Cake, 30

Ginger Spice Cake with Ginger
Glaze, 8

Pineapple Pudding Cakes, 18

Tres Leches Cake, 70

Caprese Salad Stuffed Tomatoes, 56

Caramel Coconut Cream Pie, 184

Carrots

Carrot and Parsnip Au Gratin, 16

Summer Rolls, 238

Casserole, Ham Skillet, 22

Catfish Cakes, Cajun, with Creamy
Remoulade, 38

Chamomile Cooler, 280

Cheese

Asparagus and Tomato Tart, 136

Baked Mashed Potatoes, 154

Cajun Quesadilla, 42

Caprese Salad Stuffed
Tomatoes, 56

Carrot and Parsnip Au Gratin, 16

Cheesy Creamed Spinach, 170

Cuban Sandwiches with Plantain
Chips, 69

Eggplant Rollatini, 87

Grilled Margherita Pizza, 62

Ham and Cheese Breakfast
Burritos, 282

Ham and Cheese Soufflé, 28

Lasagna Roll-Ups, 206

Pork Nachos, 98

Pork Parmesan, 248

Portobello Burgers, 78

Sausage and Pepper Baked Ziti, 118

Savory Noodle Pie, 208

Spinach and Cheese Soufflé, 176

Steak and Cheese Hoagies, 224

Veggie Lasagna, 82

Cheesy Creamed Spinach, 170

Cherries Jubilee Ice Cream
Parfait, 40

Chicken

Arroz con Pollo, 68

Basil Chicken, 232

Cajun Quesadilla, 42

Chicken Cutlet Sandwich with Herb
Mayonnaise, 264

Chicken Jambalaya, 38

Chicken Satay with Grilled Vegetable Couscous, 114

Chicken Schnitzel with Mushroom
Sauce, 102

Chicken Sliders with Spicy BBQ
Mayo, 126

Chicken Tacos with Cucumber
Salsa, 130

Coconut Chicken Soup, 237

Grilled Chicken and Apple
Wraps, 196

Light and Crispy Fried Chicken
with Collard Greens, 242

Spicy and Sweet Chicken
Wraps, 120

Spicy Grilled Lemon Chicken, 192

Chili, Beanless Beef, 254

Chocolate

Crunchy Coated Chocolate
Truffles, 278

S'mores Pudding Parfait, 226

Cilantro Sauce, Creamy, Rice Cakes with, 73

Clam Sauce, Spaghetti with, 204

Coconut

Coconut Caramel Cream Pie, 184

Coconut Chicken Soup, 237

Coconut Flan with Crispy Coconut Cookies, 94–95

Rice Pudding with Coconut Milk, 235

Coffee Cake, 30

Collard Greens, Light and Crispy Fried Chicken with, 242

Cookies, Crispy Coconut, Coconut Flan with, 94–95

Corn

Corn Puddings, 272

Corn Salad, 266

Grilled Corn and Bean Salsa with Oven-Baked Corn Chips, 92–93

Pork Nachos, 98

Corn bread

Pork Corn Bread Bites, 260

Spicy Corn Bread, 256

Corn chips

Grilled Corn and Bean Salsa with Oven-Baked Corn Chips, 92–93

Pork Nachos, 98

Couscous

Chicken Satay with Grilled Vegeta-ble Couscous, 114

Couscous Stuffed Tomatoes, 228

Shrimp Scampi over Pesto Couscous, 222

Spicy Couscous, 182

Cranberry Orange Ho-Ho-Jitos, 172

Cream of Asparagus Soup, 144

Crispy Baby Potato Bites with Sour Cream and Bacon, 124

Crispy Wonton Cups with Tuna Salad, 277

Crunchy Coated Chocolate Truffles, 278

Cuban Mojito, 72

Cuban Sandwiches with Plantain Chips, 69

Cucumbers

Chicken Tacos with Cucumber Salsa, 130

Cucumber Cups Stuffed with Shrimp Cocktail, 128

Garlicky Hummus and Cucumber Sandwich, 265

Summer Rolls, 238

Tomato, Cucumber, and White Bean Salad, 273

Custard

Berry Custard Pie, 84

Eggnog Custard Cups, 172

D

Daiquiris

Banana Daiquiri, 225

Strawberry Orange Daiquiri, 83

Desserts

Banana Pudding, 246

Berry Custard Pie, 84

Bread Pudding, 146

Cherries Jubilee Ice Cream Parfait, 40

Coconut Caramel Cream Pie, 184

Coconut Flan with Crispy Coconut Cookies, 94–95

Coffee Cake, 30

Crunchy Coated Chocolate Truffles, 278

Eggnog Custard Cups, 172

Ginger Spice Cake with Ginger Glaze, 8

Grilled Fruit Skewers with Sweet Yogurt Sauce, 116

Pear Strudel, 106

Pineapple Pudding Cakes, 18

Pumpkin Mousse, 156

Rice Pudding with Coconut Milk, 235

S'mores Pudding Parfait, 226

Tres Leches Cake, 70

Walnut Raisin Tarts, 214

White Chocolate-Chip Shortcake with Basil Strawberries, 58

Dips

Bean Dip, 247

Eggplant Dip, 219

Donuts, Mini Apple Spice Glazed, 140

Drinks

Banana Daiquiri, 225

Bloody Mary, 31

Chamomile Cooler, 280

Cranberry Orange Ho-Ho-Jitos, 172

Cuban Mojito, 72

Frosty Sparkling Apple Cider, 105

Gentle Hurricane Cocktail, 39

Iced Ginger Green Tea, 195

Mango Margarita, 256

Orange Basil Bellinis, 203

Pineapple Paradise, 20

Pumpkin Pie Martini, 158

Put a Stick in It Cocktail, 117

Raspberry Lemonade, 270

Raspberry Orange Slushies, 194

Rosemary Lemon Spritzer, 216

Sparkling Cider Mimosa, 142

Sparkling Spritzer Bar, 129

Strawberry Orange Daiquiri, 83

Sweet Tea Cocktail, 245

Thai Iced Tea, 236

Watermelon Martini, 60

Dumplings

German Dumpling Soup, 109

Parsley Dumplings (Spaetzle), 104

E

Edamame

Bow Ties and Buttons, 187

Pan-Fried Tilapia with Sautéed
Edamame, 180

Eggnog Custard Cups, 172

Eggplant

Eggplant Dip, 219

Eggplant Rollatini, 87

Moussaka, 212

Veggie Lasagna, 82

Eggs

Eggs Benedict, 26

Eggs in Purgatory, 33

Farmhouse Hash with Poached
Eggs, 48

Ham and Cheese Breakfast Burritos, 282

Ham and Egg Tea Sandwiches, 276

Niçoise Salad with Lemon Garlic
Vinaigrette, 280

Spaghetti Carbonara, 202

Spinach and Potato Frittata, 47

Entrées

Arroz con Pollo, 68

Asparagus and Tomato Tart, 136

Basil Chicken, 232

Beanless Beef Chili, 254

Beef Kebabs, 182

Cajun Catfish Cakes with Creamy
Remoulade, 36

Chicken Cutlet Sandwich with Herb
Mayonnaise, 264

Chicken Jambalaya, 38

Chicken Satay with Grilled Vegetable Couscous, 114

Chicken Schnitzel with Mushroom
Sauce, 102

Chicken Sliders with Spicy BBQ
Mayo, 126

Crispy Wonton Cups with Tuna
Salad, 277

Cuban Sandwiches with Plantain
Chips, 69

Eggs Benedict, 26

Farmhouse Hash with Poached
Eggs, 48

French Toast with Brown-Sugar
Banana Syrup, 138

Fried Pork Chops with Buttered
Beans, 244

Garlicky Hummus and Cucumber
Sandwich, 265

Ginger and Brown Sugar Glazed
Ham, 14

Grilled Corn and Bean Salsa with
Oven-Baked Corn Chips, 92–93

Grilled Pork Chops with Peach
Salsa, 54

Grilled Tex-Mex Pork Chops, 252

Ham and Cheese Soufflé, 28

Ham and Egg Tea Sandwiches, 276

Light and Crispy Fried Chicken
with Collard Greens, 242

Moussaka, 212

Pan-Fried Tilapia with Sautéed
Edamame, 180

Pork Parmesan, 248

Pork Ragu over Penne, 200

Portobello Burgers, 78

Roast Bone-in Pork Loin with Apple Mustard Glaze, 166

Roasted Turkey Breast with Spicy
Herb Oil, 150

Sausage and Pepper Skewers with
Grilled Polenta, 112

Savory Bread Pudding with
Sausage and Mushrooms, 46

Shrimp Scampi over Pesto
Couscous, 222

Slow-Cooked Orange Pork-
Shoulder Tacos with Cabbage
Slaw, 90

Slow Cooker Short Ribs, 4

Spaghetti Carbonara, 202

Spaghetti with Clam Sauce, 204

Spicy Grilled Lemon Chicken, 192

Spinach and Pasta Pie, 213

Spinach and Potato Frittata, 47

Steak and Cheese Hoagies, 224

Steamed Mahi Mahi with
Vegetables and Garlic Mustard
Sauce, 190

Veggie Lasagna, 82

Zucchini Cakes, 80

Entrées (Round 2 Recipes)

Beef and Bean Burritos, 258

Beef Kebab Pita Pockets, 186

Black Bean and Pork Stew, 74

Bow Ties and Buttons, 187

Cajun Quesadilla, 42

Chicken Tacos with Cucumber
Salsa, 130

Eggplant Rollatini, 87

Eggs in Purgatory, 33

Farmhouse Hash Taquitos, 51

Fried Bread Pudding Bites, 50

Grilled Chicken and Apple
Wraps, 196

Grilled Margherita Pizza, 62

Ham and Cheese Breakfast
Burritos, 282

Ham Skillet Casserole, 22

Lasagna Roll-Ups, 206

Pork Corn Bread Bites, 260

Pork Hash, 174

Pork Nachos, 98

Potato and Shrimp Salad with Sour
Cream and Bacon Dressing, 132

Pulled Pork Sliders with Mustard
BBQ Sauce and Pickled
Onions, 96

Rice Cakes with Creamy Cilantro
Sauce, 73

Sausage and Pepper Baked
Ziti, 118

Savory Bread Pudding with
Ham, 32

Savory Noodle Pie, 208

Spicy and Sweet Chicken
Wraps, 120

Spinach and Cheese Soufflé, 176

Spinach and Mushroom Pasta, 218

Stuffed Peppers, 196

Stuffed Zucchini Boats, 86

F

Farmhouse Hash Taquitos, 51

Farmhouse Hash with Poached Eggs, 48

Fish

Cajun Catfish Cakes with Creamy
Remoulade, 36

Pan-Fried Tilapia with Sautéed
Edamame, 180

Steamed Mahi Mahi with
Vegetables and Garlic Mustard
Sauce, 190

See also Shellfish

Flan, Coconut, with Crispy Coconut
Cookies, 94–95

French Toast with Brown-Sugar Banana Syrup, 138

Fried Pork Chops with Buttered
Beans, 244

Fried Potato Cakes, 162

Fried Bread Pudding Bites, 50

Frittata, Spinach and Potato, 47

Frosty Sparkling Apple
Cider, 105

Fruit

Grilled Fruit Skewers with Sweet
Yogurt Sauce, 116

See also specific fruits

G

Garlic

Garlicky Hummus and Cucumber
Sandwich, 265

Niçoise Salad with Lemon Garlic
Vinaigrette, 280

Steamed Mahi Mahi with
Vegetables and Garlic Mustard
Sauce, 190

Gentle Hurricane Cocktail, 39

German Dumpling Soup, 109

Ginger

Ginger and Brown Sugar Glazed
Ham, 14

Ginger Spice Cake with Ginger
Glaze, 8

Iced Ginger Green Tea, 195

Golden Raisin and Walnut
Stuffing, 152

Grilled Chicken and Apple
Wraps, 196

Grilled Corn and Bean Salsa with
Oven-Baked Corn Chips,
92–93

Grilled Fruit Skewers with Sweet Yogurt Sauce, 116

Grilled Margherita Pizza, 62

Grilled Pork Chops with Peach
Salsa, 54

Grilled Tex-Mex Pork Chops, 252

H

Ham

Ginger and Brown Sugar Glazed
Ham, 14

Ham and Cheese Breakfast Burritos, 282

Ham and Cheese Soufflé, 28

Ham and Egg Tea Sandwiches, 276

Ham Skillet Casserole, 22

Savory Bread Pudding with Ham,
32

Hash

Farmhouse Hash Taquitos, 51

Farmhouse Hash with Poached
Eggs, 48

Pork Hash, 174

Ho-Ho-Jitos, Cranberry Orange, 172

Hollandaise Sauce, 26

Hummus, Garlicky, and Cucumber Sandwich, 265

Hurricane Cocktail, Gentle, 39

I

Ice Cream Parfait, Cherries Jubilee, 40

Iced Ginger Green Tea, 195

L

Lasagna

Lasagna Roll-Ups, 206

Veggie Lasagna, 82

Lemon

Blueberry Scones with Lemon Glaze, 268

Niçoise Salad with Lemon Garlic Vinaigrette, 280

Raspberry Lemonade, 270

Rosemary Lemon Spritzer, 216

Spicy Grilled Lemon Chicken, 192

Light and Crispy Fried Chicken with Collard Greens, 242

M

Mahi Mahi, Steamed, with Vegetables and Garlic Mustard Sauce, 190

Mango Margarita, 256

Margherita Pizza, Grilled, 62

Martinis

Pumpkin Pie Martini, 158

Watermelon Martini, 60

Mimosa, Sparkling Cider, 142

Mini Apple Spice Glazed Donuts, 140

Mixed Roasted Potatoes with Herb Butter, 168

Mojito, Cuban, 72

Moussaka, 212

Mousse, Pumpkin, 156

Mushrooms

Beef and Mushroom Soup, 10

Brown Rice and Mushroom Salad, 191

Chicken Schnitzel with Mushroom Sauce, 102

Mushroom Walnut Tarts, 6

Portobello Burgers, 78

Savory Bread Pudding with Sausage and Mushrooms, 46

Spinach and Mushroom Pasta, 218

Steamed Mahi Mahi with Vegetables and Garlic Mustard Sauce, 190

Stuffed Zucchini Boats, 86

Mustard

Pulled Pork Sliders with Mustard BBQ Sauce and Pickled Onions, 96

Roast Bone-in Pork Loin with Apple Mustard Glaze, 166

Steamed Mahi Mahi with Vegetables and Garlic Mustard Sauce, 190

N

Nachos, Pork, 98

Niçoise Salad with Lemon Garlic Vinaigrette, 280

Noodles

Pad Thai, 234

Summer Rolls, 238

See also Pasta

O

Onions, Pickled, Pulled Pork Sliders with Mustard BBQ Sauce and, 96

Orange

Cranberry Orange Ho-Ho-Jitos, 172

Grilled Fruit Skewers with Sweet Yogurt Sauce, 116

Orange Basil Bellinis, 203

Raspberry Orange Slushies, 194

Slow-Cooked Orange Pork-Shoulder Tacos with Cabbage Slaw, 90

Strawberry Orange Daiquiri, 83

Orzo

Caprese Salad Stuffed Tomatoes, 56

Orzo Soup with Pork, 64

P

Pad Thai, 234

Pan-Fried Tilapia with Sautéed Edamame, 180

Parfaits

Cherries Jubilee Ice Cream
Parfait, 40

S'mores Pudding Parfait, 226

Parsley Dumplings (Spaetzle), 104

Parsnip and Carrot Au Gratin, 16

Pasta

Bow Ties and Buttons, 187

Lasagna Roll-Ups, 206

Pork Ragu over Penne, 200

Sausage and Pepper Baked Ziti, 118

Savory Noodle Pie, 208

Spaghetti Carbonara, 202

Spaghetti with Clam Sauce, 204

Spinach and Mushroom Pasta, 218

Spinach and Pasta Pie, 213

Veggie Lasagna, 82

Peach Salsa, Grilled Pork Chops
with, 54

Peanut Dipping Sauce, 238

Pears

Cabbage and Pear Slaw, 108

Pear Strudel, 106

Peas, snow

Crispy Wonton Cups with Tuna
Salad, 277

Niçoise Salad with Lemon Garlic
Vinaigrette, 280

Penne, Pork Ragu over, 200

Peppers, bell

Chicken Satay with Grilled
Vegetable Couscous, 114

Sausage and Pepper Skewers with
Grilled Polenta, 112

Stuffed Peppers, 196

Veggie Lasagna, 82

Pesto

Basil Walnut Pesto, 82

Shrimp Scampi over Pesto
Couscous, 222

Pies

Berry Custard Pie, 84

Coconut Caramel Cream Pie, 184

Savory Noodle Pie, 208

Spinach and Pasta Pie, 213

Pineapple

Grilled Fruit Skewers with Sweet
Yogurt Sauce, 116

Pineapple Paradise, 20

Pineapple Pudding Cakes, 18

Pita Pockets, Beef Kebab, 186

Pizza, Grilled Margherita, 62

Plantain Chips, Cuban Sandwiches
with, 69

Polenta, Grilled, Sausage and Pepper
Skewers with, 112

Pork

Black Bean and Pork Stew, 74

Cuban Sandwiches with Plantain
Chips, 69

Fried Pork Chops with Buttered
Beans, 244

Grilled Pork Chops with Peach
Salsa, 54

Grilled Tex-Mex Pork Chops, 252

Orzo Soup with Pork, 64

Pork Corn Bread Bites, 260

Pork Hash, 174

Pork Nachos, 98

Pork Parmesan, 248

Pork Ragu over Penne, 200

Pulled Pork Sliders with Mustard
BBQ Sauce and Pickled
Onions, 96

Roast Bone-in Pork Loin with Apple Mustard Glaze, 166

Slow-Cooked Orange Pork-
Shoulder Tacos with Cabbage
Slaw, 90

Portobello Burgers, 78

Potatoes

Baked Mashed Potatoes, 154

Crispy Baby Potato Bites with Sour
Cream and Bacon, 124

Farmhouse Hash Taquitos, 51

Farmhouse Hash with Poached
Eggs, 48

Fried Potato Cakes, 162

Mixed Roasted Potatoes with Herb
Butter, 168

Pork Hash, 174

Potato and Shrimp Salad with Sour
Cream and Bacon Dressing, 132

Spinach and Potato Frittata, 47

Puddings

Banana Pudding, 246

Bread Pudding, 146

Corn Puddings, 272

Fried Bread Pudding Bites, 50

Pineapple Pudding Cakes, 18

Rice Pudding with Coconut
Milk, 235

Savory Bread Pudding with
Ham, 32

Savory Bread Pudding with
Sausage and Mushrooms, 46

S'mores Pudding Parfait, 226

Pulled Pork Sliders with Mustard
BBQ Sauce and Pickled
Onions, 96

Pumpkin

Pumpkin Mousse, 156

Pumpkin Pie Martini, 158

Put a Stick in It Cocktail, 117

Q

Quesadilla, Cajun, 42

R

Raisins
Golden Raisin and Walnut
Stuffing, 152
Walnut Raisin Tarts, 214

Raspberries
Berry Custard Pie, 84
Raspberry Lemonade, 270
Raspberry Orange Slushies, 194
Red Cabbage Slaw, 90
Remoulade, Creamy, Cajun Catfish
Cakes with, 36

Rice
Arroz con Pollo, 68
Basil Chicken, 232
Brown Rice and Mushroom
Salad, 191
Cajun Red Bean and Rice Soup, 42
Chicken Jambalaya, 38
Rice Cakes with Creamy Cilantro
Sauce, 73
Rice Pudding with Coconut Milk, 235
Stuffed Peppers, 196
Roast Bone-in Pork Loin with Apple
Mustard Glaze, 166
Roasted Turkey Breast with Spicy
Herb Oil, 150
Rosemary Lemon Spritzer, 216

S

Salads
Brown Rice and Mushroom
Salad, 191

Caprese Salad Stuffed
Tomatoes, 56
Corn Salad, 266
Crispy Wonton Cups with Tuna
Salad, 277
Niçoise Salad with Lemon Garlic
Vinaigrette, 280
Potato and Shrimp Salad with Sour
Cream and Bacon Dressing, 132
Tomato, Cucumber, and White
Bean Salad, 273

Salsa
Chicken Tacos with Cucumber
Salsa, 130
Grilled Corn and Bean Salsa with
Oven-Baked Corn Chips, 92–93
Grilled Pork Chops with Peach
Salsa, 54

Sandwiches
Beef Kebab Pita Pockets, 186
Chicken Cutlet Sandwich with Herb
Mayonnaise, 264
Chicken Sliders with Spicy BBQ
Mayo, 126
Cuban Sandwiches with Plantain
Chips, 69
Garlicky Hummus and Cucumber
Sandwich, 265
Ham and Egg Tea Sandwiches, 276
Pork Parmesan, 248
Portobello Burgers, 78
Pulled Pork Sliders with Mustard
BBQ Sauce and Pickled
Onions, 96
Steak and Cheese Hoagies, 224

Sauces
Aioli Sauce, 78
Basil Walnut Pesto, 82
Creamy Cilantro Sauce, 73

Hollandaise Sauce, 26
Mustard BBQ Sauce, 96
Peanut Dipping Sauce, 238

Sausage
Farmhouse Hash Taquitos, 51
Farmhouse Hash with Poached
Eggs, 48
Sausage and Pepper Baked Ziti, 118
Sausage and Pepper Skewers with
Grilled Polenta, 112
Savory Bread Pudding with
Sausage and Mushrooms, 46
Savory Bread Pudding with Ham, 32
Savory Bread Pudding with Sausage
and Mushrooms, 46
Savory Noodle Pie, 208
Scones, Blueberry, with Lemon
Glaze, 268

Shellfish
Cucumber Cups Stuffed with
Shrimp Cocktail, 128
Potato and Shrimp Salad with
Sour Cream and Bacon
Dressing, 132
Shrimp Bruschetta, 228
Shrimp Scampi over Pesto Cous-
cous, 222
Spaghetti with Clam Sauce, 204
Shortcake, White Chocolate-Chip,
with Basil Strawberries, 58

Shrimp
Cucumber Cups Stuffed with
Shrimp Cocktail, 128
Potato and Shrimp Salad with
Sour Cream and Bacon
Dressing, 132
Shrimp Bruschetta, 228
Shrimp Scampi over Pesto
Couscous, 222

Side dishes

Baked Mashed Potatoes, 154

Brown Rice and Mushroom
Salad, 191

Caprese Salad Stuffed
Tomatoes, 56

Carrot and Parsnip Au Gratin, 16

Corn Salad, 266

Golden Raisin and Walnut
Stuffing, 152

Grilled Corn and Bean Salsa
with Oven-Baked Corn
Chips, 92–93

Mixed Roasted Potatoes with Herb
Butter, 168

Mushroom Walnut Tarts, 6

Pad Thai, 234

Parsley Dumplings (Spaetzle), 104

Spicy Corn Bread, 256

Spicy Couscous, 182

Zucchini Cakes, 80

Side dishes (Round 2 Recipes)

Bow Ties and Buttons, 187

Cabbage and Pear Slaw, 108

Corn Puddings, 272

Fried Potato Cakes, 162

Fried Bread Pudding Bites, 50

Rice Cakes with Creamy Cilantro
Sauce, 73

Spinach and Cheese Soufflé, 176

Slow-Cooked Orange Pork-
Shoulder Tacos with Cab-
bage Slaw, 90

Slow Cooker Short Ribs, 4

S'mores Pudding Parfait, 226

Soufflés

Ham and Cheese Soufflé, 28

Spinach and Cheese Soufflé, 176

Soups

Beef and Mushroom Soup, 10

Cajun Red Bean and Rice Soup, 42

Coconut Chicken Soup, 237

Cream of Asparagus Soup, 144

German Dumpling Soup, 109

Orzo Soup with Pork, 64

Turkey Soup, 160

Sour Cream

Crispy Baby Potato Bites with Sour
Cream and Bacon, 124

Potato and Shrimp Salad with Sour
Cream and Bacon Dressing, 132

Spiced Sour Cream, 254

Spaghetti

Spaghetti Carbonara, 202

Spaghetti with Clam Sauce, 204

Spinach and Mushroom Pasta, 218

Spinach and Pasta Pie, 213

Sparkling Cider Mimosa, 142

Sparkling Spritzer Bar, 129

Spiced Sour Cream, 254

Spicy and Sweet Chicken Wraps, 120

Spicy Corn Bread, 256

Spicy Couscous, 182

Spicy Grilled Lemon Chicken, 192

Spinach

Cheesy Creamed Spinach, 170

Spinach and Cheese Soufflé, 176

Spinach and Mushroom Pasta, 218

Spinach and Pasta Pie, 213

Spinach and Potato Frittata, 47

Squash

Chicken Satay with Grilled
Vegetable Couscous, 114

Steamed Mahi Mahi with
Vegetables and Garlic Mustard
Sauce, 190

Stuffed Zucchini Boats, 86

Veggie Lasagna, 82

Zucchini Cakes, 80

Steak and Cheese Hoagies, 224

Steamed Mahi Mahi with Vegetables
and Garlic Mustard Sauce, 190

Stew, Black Bean and Pork, 74

Strawberries

Grilled Fruit Skewers with Sweet
Yogurt Sauce, 116

Strawberry Orange Daiquiri, 83

White Chocolate-Chip Shortcake
with Basil Strawberries, 58

Strudel, Pear, 106

Stuffed Peppers, 196

Stuffed Zucchini Boats, 86

Summer Rolls, 238

Sweet Tea Cocktail, 245

T

Tacos

Chicken Tacos with Cucumber
Salsa, 130

Slow-Cooked Orange Pork-
Shoulder Tacos with Cabbage
Slaw, 90

Taquitos, Farmhouse Hash, 51

Tarts

Asparagus and Tomato Tart, 136

Mushroom Walnut Tarts, 6

Walnut Raisin Tarts, 214

Tea

Chamomile Cooler, 280

Iced Ginger Green Tea, 195

Sweet Tea Cocktail, 245

Thai Iced Tea, 236

Thai Iced Tea, 236

Tilapia, Pan-Fried, with Sautéed
Edamame, 180

Tomatoes

Arroz con Pollo, 68

Asparagus and Tomato Tart, 136

Beanless Beef Chili, 254

Caprese Salad Stuffed Tomatoes, 56

Chicken Jambalaya, 38

Couscous Stuffed Tomatoes, 228

Cucumber Cups Stuffed with
Shrimp Cocktail, 128

Eggplant Rollatini, 87

Eggs in Purgatory, 33

Grilled Corn and Bean Salsa with
Oven-Baked Corn Chips, 92–93

Grilled Margherita Pizza, 62

Grilled Tex-Mex Pork Chops, 252

Moussaka, 212

Pork Parmesan, 248

Pork Ragu over Penne, 200

Sausage and Pepper Baked Ziti, 118

Savory Noodle Pie, 208

Shrimp Bruschetta, 228

Stuffed Peppers, 196

Tomato, Cucumber, and White
Bean Salad, 273

Tortillas

Beef and Bean Burritos, 258

Cajun Quesadilla, 42

Farmhouse Hash Taquitos, 51

Grilled Chicken and Apple
Wraps, 196

Grilled Corn and Bean Salsa with
Oven-Baked Corn Chips, 92–93

Ham and Cheese Breakfast
Burritos, 282

Slow-Cooked Orange Pork-
Shoulder Tacos with Cabbage
Slaw, 90

Tres Leches Cake, 70

Truffles, Crunchy Coated
Chocolate, 278

Tuna

Crispy Wonton Cups with Tuna
Salad, 277

Niçoise Salad with Lemon Garlic
Vinaigrette, 280

Turkey

Roasted Turkey Breast with Spicy
Herb Oil, 150

Turkey Soup, 160

V

Vegetables

Chicken Satay with Grilled
Vegetable Couscous, 114

Steamed Mahi Mahi with
Vegetables and Garlic Mustard
Sauce, 190

See also specific vegetables

Veggie Lasagna, 82

Vinaigrette, Lemon Garlic, 280

W

Walnuts

Basil Walnut Pesto, 82

Golden Raisin and Walnut
Stuffing, 152

Mushroom Walnut Tarts, 6

Walnut Raisin Tarts, 214

Watermelon Martini, 60

Whipped Cream Topping, 246

White Chocolate-Chip Shortcake
with Basil Strawberries, 58

Wonton Cups, Crispy, with Tuna
Salad, 277

Y

Yogurt Sauce, Sweet, Grilled Fruit
Skewers with, 116

Z

Ziti, Sausage and Pepper Baked, 118

Zucchini

Chicken Satay with Grilled
Vegetable Couscous, 114

Steamed Mahi Mahi with
Vegetables and Garlic Mustard
Sauce, 190

Stuffed Zucchini Boats, 86

Zucchini Cakes, 80